# STORIES OF
# HOPE

An anthology
of the redeeming hope found in Jesus

# STORIES OF HOPE

Copyright © 2021 by Luis Palau Association

ISBN 978-1-7373032-0-6

**PUBLISHED BY:**
Palau Publishing
PO Box 50
Portland, Oregon
97207

Cover design and layout: Katie Bredemeier
Art direction: Wendy Palau

Printed in the United States of America
21 22 23 24 25 // PP // 9 8 7 6 5 4 3 2 1

Stories compiled by

# WENDY PALAU

# CONTENTS

# MORE THAN
# WISHFUL THINKING

WENDY

Hope is a common word. I use it often, mostly for trivial things. I hope it doesn't rain. I hope the store is still open. I hope this cookie will taste good.

We use the word hope for important things as well. I hope my son gets the job. I hope the cancer goes away. I hope the economy improves.

Hope is a different kind of expectation for something good. The feeling that what we dream of is attainable, or that events will turn out for the best.

Hope is an emotion—a necessary emotion for a flourishing life. But it's also a verb. To look forward to something with desire and reasonable confidence. To believe. To trust. You are not uninvolved; there's an action related to it.

Psychologists tell us that without hope people find themselves in very dark places. We can lose our will to persevere…even to live! It's a dangerous thing to lose hope, to lose all ability to believe there is something good ahead.

Hope is essential for human existence. Think of your own life journey. I have had times when I have felt hopeless—when I couldn't map a pathway in my brain for how the circumstances could work out for the better. I've had times of grief...when hopeless thoughts overwhelmed me.

What do we need in these times? When we can't see a way ahead that will be better, or brighter, or happier, or purposeful? What happens when the things we've put our trust in prove to be baseless? When the people who were supposed to love and protect us don't? When they actually do the opposite and hurt us? When we experience abandonment and betrayal? When we suffer abuse and cruel people gain control? When we suffer aching disappointment and unfulfilled dreams?

I believe...as do all the contributors in this book...that hope is different from wishful thinking. True rock-solid hope is much different.

When my young daughter says to me on a bright September day, "I hope it snows today!" That is wishful thinking. She's longing for something she thinks will make her life better in that moment. "What will make my day amazing?" she thinks, "I know! Snow! I hope it snows."

I love my daughter's beautiful enthusiasm.

But rock-solid hope is something different altogether. It's real. It's attainable. And it's found in a particular person. In God himself.

There is a story in the Bible that talks about this hope. Many stories, in fact. But one in particular has always had a deep, profound impact on me. It's about a woman. A broken woman. The story tells us she has been bleeding for 12 years. For us, as women, we know exactly what that is all about. If we try, we can almost imagine the implications of such a condition, especially in an ancient culture where a woman's time of bleeding was considered unclean. She was made an outcast from the community.

The account tells us she had spent all she had on doctors. And sadly, no one could help her. Then, here comes this person. A teacher. A rabbi. He is on his way to the house of a very important man to help his sick 12-year-old daughter. Think of that. As long as this girl had been alive, this woman had been hopelessly bleeding.

As Jesus is on his way, the woman says to herself, "If only I could touch his robe, I will be healed."

And she does. She reaches out, in the midst of a great crowd, and touches the edge of Jesus' cloak. And just as she thought, she was healed! In an instant. She saw him—this teacher—and she put her hope in him. And the result was healing.

Immediately, Jesus recognizes what has happened and he notices the woman. And his response is so beautiful. He calls her daughter.

This unclean, poor, desperate woman meets Jesus and he calls her daughter—his beloved, precious child.

As he is on his way to heal a precious, loved child, he calls an unclean, poor, and desperate woman his daughter.

That is what the stories in this book are all about. These precious stories are from women all around the world. These stories are their experiences...in all honesty and humility... that they wanted to share with you.

Each story is very different. Each life circumstance unique. Painful and confusing circumstances. Each from different backgrounds and different parts of the world. Each woman has a different reason for losing hope, and each of these amazing women made a decision to follow Jesus. To reach out and touch his cloak. And in turn, they found true healing.

My prayer is that these stories will revive you. That they will fill you with hope. I also pray you'll identify with at least one of these women and realize your story is not over. Your story is important and precious.

My desire for you is that you hear the invitation of Jesus. That you would hear him calling out to you—calling you his precious daughter—and that you would respond personally. That you will reach out to him...because he is reaching out to you.

My prayer is that you will become a woman of hope today!

# THE ONE
# BEYOND THE CEILING

KRISTIN

Two questions had haunted my life for as long as I could remember…

*"Is God real?"*
*"How would I ever know for sure?"*

I grew up in a fundamental church with a strong Christian family. My grandfather, being a singing evangelist, pastor, and the patriarch of our family, directed all of us throughout our lives. Christian school, Christian scouts, Christian concerts, Christian camp meetings, weekly church attendance, and constant potlucks. These were the rituals of my childhood.

And yet, I wrestled with doubts about God's very existence.

As a young girl, I remember listening to sermons in church, twirling my mother's wedding ring around and around her finger, wondering, "Are these true stories, or just fairy tales from an old book?"

During my elementary years, I would sometimes sit in the car parked in our garage, asking God to show himself to me.

"If you are real and if you can hear me," I would say, "please open the garage door. If I can see you are real, I will believe."

Nothing ever happened.

One year, my middle-school Bible class voted to get baptized together as a group. The vote was nearly unanimous—except me. Though the peer pressure was daunting, I just couldn't do it. I couldn't take a vow I didn't fully believe. I saw no proof. So, I watched from the pew as my entire class was baptized, including my twin sister. I couldn't help but feel like the black sheep of the class, the church, and worst of all, my family.

These moments polka-dot my childhood memories. I had a wonderful family, and my heart longed to believe like they did, but I ached with doubt. It wasn't just the lack of proof, either. It was the contradictions. The phrase "Jesus loves you" collided with words like "eternal damnation." It created great confusion in my young life.

Then, when I was 14, my childhood began to crumble.

My mother got sick. It was brain cancer. I watched in horror, along with my family, as our mother physically melted away slowly before our eyes. For the next three years, I watched my family pray. I watched my grandfather bring the church elders to anoint her and cry out for healing. Feeling helpless, I wanted to take some kind of action. I clung to my mustard-seed faith and begged God to spare my beloved mom.

She died. I was devastated.

My twin sister grew closer to God during this time, but I had a very different reaction. I was angry. I literally looked up to the sky, stretched out my middle finger and screamed distinct curses at God. I decided on that day it was all a myth, and I chose to no longer believe. How could a God who was supposed to be loving and kind—and who healed people all the time in the Bible—not answer a child's prayers? I wasn't asking for a new car on my 16th birthday. *I just wanted my mom.*

A life without God meant I had to do it on my own. *I was up for the challenge.* For the next ten years, I chased the "American Dream." My arrogance grew as I began to conquer each of my life's goals. The month I graduated Summa Cum Laude from the University of Oregon, I also got married and launched two businesses with my new husband. During these ten years, we grew both our businesses, purchased a house, and had two children.

Even amid those successes, I was still haunted with the question, "What do I believe?" I embarked on a quiet quest to discover if there was something "more" out there or if I would resign myself to being an atheist.

Because my Christian cocoon had left me ignorant of other belief systems, I began to research world religions for myself. I was saddened to discover they all had their own logic gaps. Believing those writings seemed to require larger steps of faith than Christianity had.

The more I studied, the more discouraged I became.

I tried other things, too. I examined philosophies and

scientific theories—even the ones found in Star Wars. And though I found some similarities in moral codes throughout the ages, I didn't discover anything I could fully embrace as truth.

Then my quest took an odd, yet refreshing turn. In my discouragement, I realized everything humans touched seemed to create more mess, more questions, and ultimately destruction.

Humans, no matter how hard they tried, seemed to be morally flawed.

I began to observe things that have not been touched by humans—such as nature. I read, watched documentaries, and took walks with the posture of a curious child and what I observed overwhelmed my senses and my mind. The wild beauty and diverse creativity of creation captivated my attention. I was deeply intrigued by the infinite complexities everywhere I looked. From the microscope to the telescope, awe grew in my heart. Like a million-piece orchestra playing the same symphony, hope began to fill my soul. I finally determined there must be some kind of "God" and the characteristics of this God could be understood by observing the masterpiece of Earth.

My mountaintop moment came when I gave birth to my first child, Madisen. An unexpected love exploded in my heart. It was different than I had ever experienced. It went beyond my ability to contain or control, and its attributes could be defined by words like "unselfish" and "self-sacrificing." I concluded this love was unique to a parent and child, and I became aware that experiencing this love was the very first time I had experienced something beyond myself—something supernatural.

At age 28, I was far beyond my peers in achievements and my life looked perfect. We sold both of our booming businesses and giggled as we wrote huge checks to pay off our new cars. I was ready to be a stay-at-home mom as my husband took an amazing corporate-level job.

That's when the nightmare began. Within one month, I found out my husband was having an affair, and my twin sister Gretchen was diagnosed with one of the deadliest forms of breast cancers, bringing that very scary C-word back into our lives. It seemed I would be losing the two closest people in my world.

There are no words that can describe my devastation. I was the type-A twin with the change-the-world personality, but I couldn't change anything. I had no answers, no solutions, and could no longer see a path ahead.

Every morning, whether I slept or not, I would ask myself, "How can I find the strength to make it through this day?" And every evening, after I said goodnight to my kids, I would fall on my bed and cry.

It was in this desperate season, where my eyes could see no hope, that my heart began to cry out for help to the most unlikely of places—the ceiling. One night, I looked up and said, "I don't know if there is a god out there who can hear me, but if you can, and if you created the earth, and if you love me like I love my children, then I desperately need your help."

Instantly, I felt an energy come into the room and the only words I can use to describe what I experienced that night were peace and deep love. In any other moment, my intellect would have taken over. But not that night. I didn't care if it was a Hindu god or Yoda, I just needed help. I needed hope.

As this feeling came upon me like a warm blanket, I fell fast asleep.

For weeks, after I put my little ones to bed, I went to my bedroom to talk to the ceiling, and every night, that presence of peace would meet me. I would often start with these words, "If you love me like I love my kids..." then I would pour out my heart, my fears, and my hurts with total transparency because, well, it was just the ceiling.

I began to talk about practical problems like the need for a job, paying bills, caring for my two toddlers, supporting my sister, etc. And then I would end my talk with, "If you love me and you're a god with powers, would you help me?"

Peace would come and I would rest.

Soon I observed a peculiar thing: solutions to my problems began appearing, one by one. Whenever it happened, my mind quickly rationalized it all as coincidence. But it kept happening. Month after month I experienced this phenomenon. My heart and mind became convinced something supernatural was interacting with my life. My prayers were being answered. But by who?

The more this happened, the more I found myself talking to this unseen benefactor. Whoever it was, this entity was starting to feel like a doting parent coming to my rescue. I felt loved.

The crescendo came one evening after a very stressful day with divorce proceedings. This part of my life felt like a heart-wrenching soap opera. However, a last-minute unforeseen change resulted in a huge, favorable outcome. I was so amazed; I couldn't wait to kiss my babies goodnight so I could talk to my ceiling "friend" about my day.

Thankfulness permeated my heart as I shared my gratitude with tears pouring down my face. I told the ceiling how loved and protected I felt. Then I asked a question I had never asked before: "Do you have a name?"

Instantly, I heard an audible voice respond, "Jesus." I was shocked, dumbfounded, and angry!

I would have been okay with any name of any god or deity, except that one.

"No, no, no! Get away from me! You're the one who killed my mom!" I collapsed on the carpet, bawling, bewildered, and heartbroken.

But he drew near to me with an overwhelming sense of comfort. It was as if I could sense him say, "I know you don't understand now, but it wasn't me who killed your mama. I deeply loved her. I was there. I wept with you."

Step by step, he came closer still.

"Just like your little ones don't understand this divorce and all the intricate details, just as you are protecting their hearts because you know their little minds could not truly understand, so too, was it then with you and me."

A few more steps forward. "I promise one day you will understand, but know I love you and I always have. I have never left you. I have been here the whole time."

As he drew near, a revelation overtook me: Jesus cared for me like I cared for my children.

Then, it made sense. God's parental love was all over the Scriptures and was fully realized in the life of Jesus. God's kids were kidnapped by sin and separated from relationship with him. And yet he loved them so much that he left his throne and came to earth to rescue us, even dying to save us, including me. Wow! That was sacrificial love!

At last, I understood Jesus' heart for me. At last, I was able to say, "I don't understand what happened to my mom, but I trust you. You have proven yourself faithful and loving to me. Forgive me for blaming you all those years. Forgive me for my sins against you. I want you in my life. I want you to be my God. I trust your love and care, and I give you my heart."

Since that night, I have never been the same, and Jesus has never stopped showing up in my life. He has never stopped meeting with me, talking to me, or revealing himself to me. I have watched him reveal himself through Scripture. I have watched him miraculously heal my sister. And, I have watched him touch and restore every single part of my life.

As I look back, I see where the change began. It was when I started talking to the God who was waiting just beyond my ceiling. And I invite you to do the same. He is there. He sees you right where you are, and he loves you. I encourage you to take that simple step of faith, seek the God who already knows you, the one who wants to rescue you. His name is Jesus.

*Kristin and her husband Mark have been married 18 years with a blended family of five children. Mark is a pastor and Kristin is the Executive Director of a non-profit which supports foster families in Oregon. "The thief comes only to steal and kill and destroy. I came that they may have life and have it abundantly" - Jesus (John 10:10, ESV).*

# LATCHKEY
# KINGS AND QUEENS

CHARLOTTE

I think I was five when I learned the word, "bastard." With all the bravado of a six-year-old know-it-all, my brother lectured, "That's what we are. Bastards."

It was the year before, with a belly full of butterflies and glee, that I put on my yellow raincoat and boots to wait on the curb for my dad to pick my brother and me up for a rare visit. *Dad. Father. Daddy*. These words possessed all the intrigue of a mythical creature—frighteningly foreign but impossibly romantic.

I did not want to wait inside. I wanted to be there in the drizzling rain to witness the first glimmer of his car's paint as it rounded the corner. An hour later the butterflies had soured. He was not coming. He simply forgot.

As my brain stitched itself together, the bright hope in my belly petrified into the coal of disappointment. Any time I dared hope, I got a sickening, searing burn that slandered, "Stupid girl. Nobody is coming for you."

And often, it was true. Nobody was coming.

Nobody came when my brother lifted and shoved me into the industrial dumpster of our low-income apartment complex. Routinely. My cases of lice far outnumbered visits from my dad.

Nobody came as my five-year-old frame squeezed behind our living room recliner to escape my brother's flailing fists. When he could not reach me with his hands, he dropped his pants and shot urine at me until I was soaked.

Nobody came when the neighbor boy led me under his bunk bed, or into a stranger's vacant truck bed, to guide my tiny hands into his pants.

At seven, the police came. My brother shattered a sliding glass door to break into an apartment on a dare. He colored all over the walls. I played lookout. We had criminal records before we'd lost all our baby teeth.

We were the latchkey kings and queens. We lost ourselves exploring sewer pipes beneath busy streets. At only four, I woke before my mother and brother, dressed up in my puffiest pink dress, sans underwear or shoes, and left home, in search of "that nice girl I played with last week." It was not even 7 AM and I was pounding on doors in search of friendship.

I knew the nooks and crannies of our complex intimately. I spent hours in the cinder block laundry room. I scratched through layers of history in coat upon coat of beige paint on its walls as I waited for my urine-soaked sheets to spin and dry. I did not know it at the time, but I had a developmental trauma disorder. And to survive I would dissociate and disconnect from my body. My nervous system had trouble hearing basic cues like, "You're hungry. You're thirsty," or "You need to pee."

The real me was like a balloon floating far above the filthy, freckled flesh that kept it alive. My body was a necessary evil. It was too tall, too heavy. *Was that why I couldn't ride on the shoulders of a doting daddy, or be tossed in the air like those squealing kids at the pool?* My hair was too red and conspicuous. *Was that why it was left knotted into a rat's nest at school instead of lovingly braided like my classmates?*

That disgusting and shameful body would not be the boss of me. I would fight its messages. Eat, sleep, hydrate, feel the pain—*no, thank you.*

I escaped the chaos and loneliness of home by pouring myself into school. By age nine, I came early to set up and stayed late to clean or help grade papers. If I could make myself useful, I might be wanted. I would have access to caring, insightful adults. I would be safe. I could even experience soaring bursts of warmth with each award and title bestowed on me. Maybe gold stars could displace the trash and the lice and pee smells. Maybe trophies could oust the worries that threatened to crush me like laundry room cinder blocks. And it worked…a little.

If a little achievement felt good, more should feel better. In my first two years of high school, anytime there was a presidential election, my name was on the ballot. And I had not lost once. The load was heavy but it meant I could spend 14 hours a day at school. I did not have to go home.

By this time, my single mom had worked hard to land a job at the United States Postal Service, where she began at the bottom rung—the graveyard shift. She slept until 10 PM to begin work at 11 PM. I had a chance to see her for less than an hour each day, as she hurried to prepare for work.

Then, an emptiness would settle over our home. My brother monopolized the midnight hours, welcoming pot-heads and their girlfriends to make our space their own.

The strike of midnight meant that I should now begin my honors homework. I popped handfuls of pills to stay awake. With the help of over-the-counter amphetamines, I could bypass sleep and temporarily force my body and its disgusting neediness into subservience.

During finals week of my freshman year, I was bone-tired. In the middle of the night, my energy waned. I was terrified of failing.

I left the computer, entered the bathroom, and for the first time, began to cut into my wrist. I told myself, "Stupid girl, this is to remind you that you were weak tonight. Nobody is coming to save you." I swallowed more pills and stayed awake for 63 hours until finals ended.

My mask remained intact. At school, I was still the gold star girl, but my family life was unraveling.

My brother attempted suicide and was admitted to a psychiatric care facility. My dad was diagnosed with an addiction to psychiatric drugs and admitted to a treatment center.

As if this soap opera litany of issues was not enough, my mom reinforced the heaviness, regularly reciting: "Charlotte, you are holding us all together. Without you, I wouldn't have a reason to live."

To the secret habits of pill-popping and cutting, I added cycles of starving and gorging and burning my arms so I could not receive an embrace without pain. By my design, the searing sting of a hug would remind me, "Do not let anyone too close. They will only let you down."

One night, I swallowed 40 pills with ambiguous desire. I did not quite want to die, but I did not want to live like this. I wanted a different life. My skin burned, flushing into a deep, bluish-red. My breath turned shallow. I looked out my bedroom window at the moon, and white beams shot up, down, left, and right, forming a clear, bright cross in the sky. Oddly, I did not feel alone and I drifted to sleep.

The next morning my body awoke like any other day but inside I felt a fragile resolve to live. I had to write it down before I wavered. That day, I confided in a couple of close friends through a letter—I made a promise to them and to myself that I would try my best to live and not die.

In those dark years, little lights gathered on the periphery. A kind woman volunteered to chaperone our student leadership workdays. She brought nourishing snacks and lifted tasks off my plate. I was invited to an evening assembly hosted by the Fellowship of Christian Athletes. It was one more excuse to not go home, so I attended. At the end of a moving talk, the guest speaker prayed a prayer, and I felt some coldness melt in my heart. I did not understand what it meant, but I filled out a card to say that I had prayed the prayer.

The next week, the kind volunteer woman called me to talk about my response card. I was so confused. She explained that she was a campus evangelist and would love the opportunity to take me out to coffee to talk about my decision. She told me that one of my best friends had also filled out the card and that together we could join a weekly Bible study to learn about Jesus. I continued to self-harm and hide the real me, but I grew to look forward to the peaceful atmosphere of the study.

Another light twinkled as a classmate passed a note during a history lecture. The note explained she had been praying and felt like God was telling her that I was hurting myself. She let me know she used to cut too, but Jesus helped her stop. I felt outed. I was a master of disguise—how could she see behind my mask? If she was telling the truth, could it be that God saw me? Could he care?

The next summer, I received an unexpected call from that classmate. She invited me to her church's youth camp. I did not have the money or the time to go but felt strangely compelled to register. On a partial scholarship, I crammed into a stinky, 15-passenger church van headed for the mountains.

In a pine-studded amphitheater, the pastor told the story of a blind man named Bartimaeus. As Jesus passed by, the beggar shouted, "Jesus, son of David, have mercy on me!" Impervious to his humiliation, the beggar could not be shut up. Jesus did not mock him or ignore him but called him over. Jesus healed him.

The pastor asked if anyone needed the mercy of Jesus. He asked if anyone was done with polite hiding and was ready to come clean with their utter weakness and inner ugliness on the chance that Jesus would make them whole.

Could I, the little girl in rain boots, waiting for a father who'd forgotten me, hazard a hope? Would I, with burns hiding beneath sleeves, be foolish enough to invite an embrace?

I rose to my feet and walked down to the altar. With a youth leader, I asked Jesus for mercy and forgiveness. And the slandering voice that taunted, "Nobody is coming for you," was silenced.

Jesus came.

"I will not leave you as orphans; I will come to you" (John 14:18).

He lifted my heavy load. He was not the one stacking bricks on tiny shoulders. He took them on himself.

"Come to me, all of you who are weary and carry heavy burdens, and I will give you rest" (Matthew 11:28, NLT).

He did not ask me to hold it all together or give him a reason to live.

"When we were utterly helpless, Christ came at just the right time and died for us sinners" (Romans 5:6, NLT).

He did not ask me to hate my body and its needs—to

despise hunger and thirst. But instead, he offered to fill me.

"I am the bread of life. Whoever comes to me will never be hungry again. Whoever believes in me will never be thirsty" (John 6:35, NLT).

In gentleness and power, he went before me, his Spirit filling the dark and dangerous places within. Like the father I never had, he went room by room displacing the accuser who had set up headquarters in my belly. He made it clear that the stubborn bear of depression would not have run of the house any longer. He made it safe for me to inhabit my body again.

I forgave my mother and led her in that simple prayer in our kitchen.

I forgave a boy who'd touched me and led him in that prayer one line at a time over Instant Messenger. He said that months before he prayed, "God, if you could forgive me of that, I trust you could forgive me of anything."

And for 18 years now, Jesus has been faithful to melt this hard heart of mine. I may have been rescued in just one moment, but I have been healed over millions of moments.

I have been healed as I felt God whisper through my ugly tears, "Let him love you," when I was terrified of the gentle goodness of a young man intent on pursuing me. I listened to Jesus and now get to witness this gentle man love our two small daughters each day.

I have been healed as ten years after meeting Jesus, I accepted his invitation to unpack the trauma still silently decaying inside me. Jesus showed up in the body of a friend who dropped everything to come over to make me chicken soup, declaring, "Your soul is feeling sick. I will take care of you."

The Father takes your abandonment and calls you beloved. Nothing can separate you from his loving care. He offers healing and freedom to every orphan who dares to believe his promise—"I will bring you safely home."

*Charlotte is married with two children. She serves with a non-profit organization working in digital media using her gifts to share hope with people around the world.*

# MY MORNING
# STAR

DARCY

As I reflect on my life, it is clear that God's fingerprints were all over me before I even knew it.

At 51-years-old, shockingly to me, I am married to a pastor. We have been in ministry, working at and leading churches, for more than 17 years now. No one could have ever anticipated Josh would be a pastor. In fact, the night I met him, he was the lead singer of a glam rock band playing in a seedy punk club in downtown Portland, Oregon. He wore leather pants, a dog chain around his neck, and heavy black eyeliner.

I, on the other hand, was into Mother Earth and crystals and enjoyed camping in the nude. Somehow our lives came together, and it was love at first sight. We were immediately convinced we were soul mates.

But I'm jumping ahead. First, I want to share some history with you. I did not grow up in church. I attended occasionally throughout my childhood, especially when I would visit my Granny, who was a devout Lutheran. But I never grasped what it meant to have a relationship with Jesus. I suppose I came to think of God as the one to go to in a crisis, but nothing more.

As I went off to college, I started delving into New Age mysticism and spirituality. It was much more appealing to me and didn't have all of the "rules" of Christianity. It felt so free and was more about discovering yourself through "enlightenment." My practices deepened as I moved into my twenties. I loved my life and my freedom.

Fast forward to 26-year-old me. I was living a vibrant, independent life in downtown Portland and my little brother —my only sibling—decided to move to San Francisco. We were incredibly close, and I thought he was the most magical person in the world—creative, joyful, and a true free spirit. As a gay man, he felt more at home in San Francisco. That Christmas, in 1994, my parents got a call that Jason was in the hospital. He had been sick for quite some time and decided to get checked out. It was at this point that he was diagnosed with an AIDS-related form of pneumonia.

My only sibling had full-blown AIDS. I can't even explain how fearful and angry I was. It was a long and painful two years, and my dear parents left their lives behind in Oregon to care for my brother for the remainder of his life.

When he died two years later, it felt as though a part of me died with him.

We had a beautiful memorial service for him in Golden Gate Park and another funeral for him in a church on the

Oregon Coast. Sitting there in the church, in the front pew, was the first time I remember believing with all my heart, "There is no God. I would never worship a God who would allow this beautiful soul to be taken from me."

Fast forward another year and a half, and I had met and married that David Bowie-esque rockstar I referenced earlier. He was signed to a major record label and we were living in Seattle. We were so full of hope for an exciting and successful future. However, in no time at all, the band was dropped from the record label, their single failed on the radio, and he was jobless. Our dreams were dashed.

One day I came home from work and found my husband reading the Bible. Honestly, I almost fell over. At that point, after losing my brother, I wanted absolutely nothing to do with Christians or God. I remember feeling outraged and disgusted at the sight of him reading the Bible.

And that was just the beginning. In the hopelessness of his situation, through reading the Bible, as well as authors such as A.W. Tozer and C.S. Lewis, and attending a local church, he found Jesus. He found hope and a community who welcomed him. All the while, I was angry and remained unconvinced of the "Good News" changing his life. It is a complete miracle we stayed married. Even though I was denying God, when I look back, it is so obvious that the Lord was already at work in my life.

A couple of years later, I was fed up. Josh professed his faith in Jesus, attended church regularly, and was even helping out on the worship team. But he was still failing as a husband. It often felt more like I was married to an irresponsible teenager! I wanted more from him. It was just confirming what I already thought—all Christians were hypocrites.

At that point, I informed him that I wanted to leave him. Even though he claimed to be a believer and loved Jesus, his focus seemed to remain on himself and his goal of being a famous rockstar.

Regardless of Josh's irresponsibility, I always knew he loved me immensely. When I threatened to leave, I saw this in action. He was a broken man. He quit his band, got a real job, and his love began to manifest in physical and emotional ways that it never had before. He was actually caring for me and putting me first. After a few weeks of seeing his love "in action," I remember thinking, "Ok. If God can actually, genuinely, change a man...maybe there is something to this God-thing."

Seeing Josh's new, more selfless love for me honestly opened me up to the love of Jesus.

I started to visit his church. I got connected to a small group of lovely women who had been walking with the Lord for a long time. They were so kind to me. I remember they used to tell me Bible stories as if I was a child, and I just couldn't get enough. They were so gentle and gracious, and they had this thing, this light, this energy, that just drew me in.

I couldn't figure out what they had but I wanted some of it.

A short time later, Josh returned from his first mission trip to Russia, began writing worship songs, and was becoming more rooted in his faith. The Lord just kept drawing me to himself, even though I didn't fully realize what was happening. I continued to spend time with the wonderful group of women who loved me unconditionally and gave me the space and time to share the questions and doubts I had about following Jesus. That's when I found out I was pregnant.

Since my brother's death in 1996, my parents had come into the most beautiful relationship with Jesus. They had joined a local church in their area in California and found a family. A family that mourned with them and walked alongside them, pointing them to Jesus, as they healed. For Easter of 2001, I went to California to visit them. At that point I was three months pregnant. Their pastor was giving a passionate sermon and calling people to come to Jesus. The last thing I remember is him saying, "If anyone wants to accept Jesus Christ as their Lord and Savior, please stand now." And without hesitation, I stood up.

My parents—and of course, Josh—were elated.

I returned home to Seattle to a new Bible Josh had bought me. I tried to read it, but it was like a foreign language. Honestly, I was so frustrated. I had accepted Jesus and did not get that "thing" my friends from church had. I wanted the light I saw in them. But I didn't feel any different. I remember feeling heartbroken over this.

In October of 2001, we had our baby boy. I was bound

and determined to feel Jesus, to meet with him, to figure out this "light" I was so desperate for. So, in the middle of the night when I would be up with my baby, I would pray for Jesus to make himself known to me.

One night these words came to me: "Lord, draw near to me and I will draw near to you."

The words seemed odd, as it was not a way of speaking that came naturally to me. But I did feel as if they had been given to me, so the phrase became my mantra for weeks. When I think back, I realize what a beautiful gift God gave me. He did end up making himself known to me and it was the wildest, most supernatural thing I have ever experienced in my life. In the middle of one of the dark, quiet nights, as I prayed my mantra, God gave me a moment. I honestly cannot even put it into words. When I think about it, it was just the briefest moment. But after that, I knew that I knew him. I knew he was real. I had experienced his presence.

When Josh saw me the next morning, he immediately wanted to know what had happened to me. When he describes it now, in his own words, he describes seeing me as radiant, almost illuminated. He could visibly see something had changed in me.

I believe God knew that after everything I had been through, I needed a supernatural event to recognize him. And when I shared my middle-of-the-night prayer with another believer, they explained to me that those words had been given to me by the Holy Spirit—they were from the Bible, the book of James, chapter 4, verse 8 which reads: "Draw near to God, and he will draw near to you" (ESV).

God was at work in my mind, my spirit, and my heart, and I didn't even know it! He could not possibly have made himself any more real to me.

One year later, I was serving in ministry. Hilarious. I had barely started reading the Bible and felt incredibly unqualified. But I was excited about knowing, loving, and walking with Jesus.

I knew he was real. I knew he loved me. I believed the Gospel.

But, I felt like an impostor. My husband was the pastor and I had just started following Jesus. I felt embarrassed, like a fraud. But I trusted him to know what was best for our life. I constantly had to remind myself that he had chosen me for the role I was in. And as crazy as it seems, I wanted God's will and his will alone for our life. I clung to this:

"And calling to him a child, he put him in the midst of them and said, 'Truly, I say to you, unless you turn and become like children, you will never enter the kingdom of heaven. Whoever humbles himself like this child is the greatest in the kingdom of heaven'" (Matthew 18:2-4, ESV).

So here I sit, writing to you, and reflecting on walking with Jesus as my Lord and Savior for the last 18 years, being in ministry alongside my husband for 17 of those years, and I see the marks of Jesus all over my entire life.

Even when I denied him over and over, he pursued me

with patience and persistence.  Even when I was outraged and hateful toward him, he loved me with gentleness and drew me closer to himself.

I want you to know God doesn't just repair our old hearts, he gives us entirely new hearts.  We are new creations in Christ when we accept Jesus into our hearts. The old life is gone, and the new life has come!

He is our guide, our Morning Star. He is with us in our suffering, our Wounded Healer. He will never leave us nor forsake us, our Good Shepherd.

He is faithful. Always.

I pray that as he woos you, you will heed his call. He offers a peace and a hope like you have never known. And as you come to know him, may you know with every ounce of your being, "Those who look to him are radiant; their faces are never covered with shame" (Psalm 34:5).

*Darcy and her husband pastor a thriving church in the urban core of Portland, Oregon, which they planted 11 years ago. They have been married 23 years and have two children. Darcy's heart is to serve women in her community.*

# THE UPRISING

My story begins in communist Romania in the mid-1970s. I was born in a small village on the Danube River. We soon moved to Timisoara, the second largest city in Romania, where I grew up as an only child in a Christian family. My parents attended a local Baptist church there. As a child, I learned about God and the Bible. However, living as Christians in a culture dictated by a communist regime was incredibly challenging.

Basic food and normal commodities that most people take for granted were sparse and difficult to obtain. We stood in line for hours for small monthly rations of flour, oil, sugar, eggs, and milk. My parents worked hard to provide for our family—dad worked day shifts as an accounting clerk in a warehouse and my mom worked night shifts as a nurse on an ambulance while taking care of me during the day.

As a country, we were closed off physically and intellectually from the rest of the world. Only two hours of television transmission were available per day. One hour was national news praising the merits of the communist party followed by another hour of some show or movie that was highly censored and portrayed socialist ideologies.

Each classroom in school displayed a picture of President Ceausescu and every morning we would start the day facing his picture and pledging allegiance to him. We lived in constant fear, and hopelessness prevailed all around. My parents told me from an early age that we do not talk about God, our faith, or our church, and we don't say anything negative about the communist government or the president to absolutely anyone. No one could really be trusted.

At school, in the first grade, all the children were asked to stand up and declare their religious affiliation. I was naïve and remembered being taught at church to always tell the truth. So, I stood and told the whole class I was a Christian Baptist. However, every other child in my class responded saying they were Christian Orthodox. The Romanian Orthodox religion was the only religious system approved by the communist regime. The Baptist church I grew up in was basically illegal. We met in secret, and if we kept quiet inside the church building no one suffered any persecution. However, I came to find out later that many who were passionate to share the Gospel of Jesus Christ outside of the church were severely persecuted, tortured, or thrown in jail; some disappeared without a trace, and some were even killed.

Upon hearing I was a Christian Baptist, my teacher summoned my parents to school immediately to discuss my answer. My parents knew they could face severe repercussions due to my response. All they could do was be honest about their faith when talking to the teacher and pray for God's protection. My teacher took a risk and changed the answer she had to report to the communist party.

Growing up in our church, I often heard the Gospel story of Jesus Christ and many other wonderful Bible stories. I learned about Jesus and how he came to die for our sins to prepare a place for us in heaven. I also was taught about how awful hell is. I remember I was terrified of going to hell if I died. The church also taught many other strict rules and had many legalistic aspects. Even though they preached that Jesus came to free us from our sins, we were required to keep many other rules. We were told to never miss a church service. As a girl, I was told to never wear pants, only dresses. I could never wear makeup or jewelry. Dancing was never allowed. Married women were told to cover their heads when in church. We were even taught that if we messed up bad enough we could lose our salvation and our status in the church.

As a child, the message my heart received was to always try hard to prove my faith by my works. I was always afraid I would break a rule, mess up, and I would not be "good enough" to be allowed into heaven. I remember praying to receive Jesus into my heart many times as a young child to assure I would go to heaven if I died. But I never had peace in my heart. I lived in constant fear and hopelessness. I never felt "good enough."

In 1989, the Romanian people started a revolution

against the communist regime. It started in my hometown of Timisoara, and it spread like a wildfire across Romania. It was a very bloody revolution and thousands who stood up to speak against the communist government were killed without mercy on the streets. As a 13-year-old at that time, I feared for my life, as well as the lives of my parents, who still had to go to work. We mostly stayed inside our apartment with no lights on at night in fear of being shot at. The country had never seen such evil, darkness, and fear before. However, a glimmer of hope was emerging out of the dark tyranny of the communist oppression the country had endured for decades.

After a long month of shootings and morgues overflowing with dead bodies, the dictator and his wife were captured and killed. Romania was finally free from the communist oppression.

The next year, as a freshman in high school, my English teacher introduced me to a Christian missionary couple from Texas living in Timisoara at the time. I spent many hours talking to them, and getting to know them. I was so hungry to hear about America and their culture. It was all so new to me and I was fascinated to hear all their stories. As we got to know each other, they helped me understand the true sacrifice Jesus paid for my sins on the cross—that it was complete and sufficient for my salvation. I learned from them that my salvation is eternal and secure because Jesus took the penalty for my sin and died in my place; it is not through my own merits or good works. The message they gave me truly had God's fingerprints all over it. It gave me such clarity, peace, and hope when I finally understood I would never be "good enough," yet Jesus' sacrifice for me was sufficient to gain my salvation. I finally understood my security in him for all eternity. There was no need to fear death any longer.

Soon thereafter, an evangelistic crusade was announced in Timisoara. The crusade was to take place in an open field soccer stadium led by a man named Luis Palau. This was un-precedented—the first time in my life that an American evan-gelist would preach the message of Jesus Christ openly outside the church! I was so excited to attend.

I listened to Luis share the unconditional love of Jesus that night with a huge crowd of thousands of other fellow Romanians. That night felt like a revival in our hometown! The Holy Spirit was present and powerfully moving hearts. Many were desperate to hear a message of love and hope after so many years of communist oppression and tyranny. At the end of the message, Luis gave an invitation to open the door of our hearts to Jesus and make a commitment to follow him for the rest of our lives. I felt the nudging of the Holy Spirit and I walked forward toward the platform where Luis was preach-ing, following his invitation. Hundreds of others joined me on the field, making the decision to follow Jesus. It truly was an incredible evening that will forever be imprinted in my memory.

From that moment on, all fear and hopelessness were gone! The wonderful love of Jesus changed my life. Now, peace and joy flooded my heart. I had assurance that if I died,

I would be with him in heaven. I was soon baptized in my local church and told everyone about my commitment to walk with Jesus for the rest of my life. I continued to grow in my faith as a young teen. I loved serving in church, singing in the youth choir, and helping others know the same love and peace I found in Jesus.

In my junior year, I remember our youth pastor challenged us to trust God with "big things" as well as "little things." He challenged us to pray consistently for "something big"—that only God could do—to trust him and watch him work.

Hearing so much from my American missionary friends about their country, I made the decision to pray that God would allow me to go to America one day. I knew financially this would be impossible for my family so I started praying and trusting God with "something big that only he could do." No one knew about this prayer. It was just between me and the Lord.

As I was approaching my senior year in high school, my American missionary friends asked me one night over dinner about my plans for college. I mentioned my plans to attend the local public university. They asked me if I would ever consider going to college in the United States. I was surprised by their question and told them that would be an impossibility. They shared with me that the Lord had put the idea of helping me go to college in the U.S. on their hearts. I was floored and could not believe my ears.

This was only the beginning of a long journey of faith in my walk with the Lord. Going to the U.S. was quite an adventure with many twists and unexpected turns. Yet a few things were consistent throughout the journey: God's faithfulness carrying me through various challenging situations, showering me with his unconditional love and grace, and his timely provision of all my needs.

Seven years later, only by God's grace, I graduated from the University of Oklahoma with a Doctor of Pharmacy degree. The Lord provided for me in truly miraculous ways to cover expenses for my education and I was blessed to graduate debt-free! The same year I married the love of my life and now we have two wonderful sons and a daughter we love so much. The Lord has truly blessed us.

Throughout my entire journey, one thing has been clear—no matter how dark or hopeless your situation might be right now, there is always hope with Jesus. He will make a way when there seems to be no way.

*Adela and her husband live in the U.S., are active in their local church, and are raising their three children to love the Lord deeply.*

# MY SO-CALLED
# FAIRY-TALE LIFE

FONDA

I was living every woman's dream. I married the love of my life, we had three darling children, and we lived in a beautiful home on the water in Ft. Lauderdale. My father-in-law had become a household name after creating three Fortune 500 companies and owning three professional sports teams. My husband and I were incredibly wealthy as well, and we were treated like royalty wherever we went. It was a life of privilege and power; we had access to nearly anything we wanted to do or buy.

This was such a radical departure from my childhood in South Florida. I was an only child in an upper middle-class family that attended church weekly. But, when I was five years old something went terribly wrong, and my parents and I left the church for good. After that, I had no desire to return, but I would occasionally attend Mass with my Catholic friends. Even though that was the extent of my religious experience, I considered myself a good person and never doubted I would go to heaven.

My father was an engineer, so from a very early age I put my faith in science and simply dismissed religious beliefs as archaic, irrelevant, or ignorant. I believed I was in complete control of my life, and to achieve my goals I would have to work incredibly hard and sacrifice the comfort of relationships. I accepted there was no one who would be there to walk that path with me, no one to pick up the pieces if I bombed out. And if I did fail, there were no second chances, it would all be over. From the day I left for college, I knew I was living with no safety net and the consequences of failure were unthinkable.

So, I threw all my effort into becoming an engineer. It took everything I had…and then some…to horsepower my way through, and I constantly battled fears of inadequacy and failure. After graduating, I accepted a job with Procter and Gamble in the food and drug manufacturing division. I loved the company and thrived there, and after a little less than four years, I was offered a promotion. But, it would require a life decision: career track or "mommy" track? Back in the 80s, this was a totally legit question that was asked for a good reason. Upwardly mobile managers in the manufacturing division would move across the country several times in their careers, and as the saying went, "wives are portable, husbands…not so much." It wasn't even a question in my mind—career track, of course! However, my manager advised me to take a few weeks and think it through, just to make sure there were no "open doors" in my past.

Well, actually…there was one.

Wayne and I dated the summer after our freshman year of high school and had remained friends ever since. Ok, truth be told, I was still very much in love with him. We had spent some time together the previous Christmas, but at that point, the timing wasn't right for either of us to start a relationship. But, because I was told to make sure there were no open doors, I decided to call and let him know that I'd be in town the next weekend. And I knew whatever he said next would determine the rest of my life. To my disbelief and joy, the "door" swung wide open. Without hesitation, he invited me to spend the weekend with him. Ten months later, I left Procter and Gamble to take a position with a biomedical company in Miami. The job paid very, very well, but the real reason I came home was to live with Wayne. My friends were mortified that there was no "significant jewelry" on my ring finger, but I didn't care what they said. I knew my life would be with him.

Three years later he proposed, and within a year we were married and starting our lives together. Wayne's father had already launched Waste Management and was busy building Blockbuster Video. Every year he generously gifted us shares of stock that seemed to appreciate exponentially, and before we knew it, we were unbelievably wealthy. We traveled the world, going wherever and whenever we wanted in the family's private aircraft. We built an enormous custom home that looked more like an exclusive resort. We had employees who managed all of the mundane parts of our lives so we didn't have to bother with anything tedious or boring. We ran all over town drinking, partying, and misbehaving badly. We rarely ever suffered the consequences of our actions; money and influence can cover up a whole lot of sin. Yeah, "cover up," as in what happens in a litter box.

The years passed; Wayne Sr. continued to create wildly successful companies and gift us more stock. He acquired three professional sports teams, and suddenly we all became the object of tremendous media attention. It was a fairy-tale life, but there was a dark side that no one saw. My beloved husband was struggling with an emptiness in his heart that just could not be filled. Travel was now an escape from the overwhelming demands of his life; the expensive toys he bought never satisfied him for very long, either. I sensed a growing heaviness in his heart, so I tried even harder to make everything perfect for him. But it was never enough. I could make him happy for a while, but I couldn't keep him happy. Worse yet, I couldn't protect our children. They never knew if their friends really liked them or just the money and the cool stuff they brought to the table. A sense of failure began to eat me alive, so I compensated by trying harder and harder to make everyone happy which inevitably led to more failure, and then even more effort.

One of the few friends we still trusted was Brad, an amazing Christian man who was the Captain of a U.S. Navy fast-attack nuclear submarine. He would bring the sub into Ft. Lauderdale whenever possible to give the crew some much-deserved shore leave. We went all out to provide activities for them. Over time, Wayne grew close to Brad and often took him on fishing trips on our boat. He recognized Brad had something he was missing…there was a quiet strength about him and a sense of peace and assurance that Wayne did not have in his life. Brad explained that Wayne had a "hole" in his heart, a God-sized hole that he was trying to fill with things that would never satisfy him. No one could be truly fulfilled until they let the Lord have his rightful place in their heart.

How does one give their heart to God? We decided that church was the answer. My beloved found one that he thought might be a good fit for us. The pastor was a scuba diver, and we loved to scuba dive. It sounded like a great idea. So, we dutifully attended church every weekend…but nothing about our lives changed because we didn't change.

Then one night Wayne was invited by some friends to a different church and asked if I wanted to go with him.

No way…that's one of those churches where people stand up and wave their hands around. Nope. Not me, buddy.

So, he went without me, and for the very first time in his life, he heard a truly scriptural sermon and a salvation message. The pastor's sermon was about what had been weighing so heavily on Wayne's heart. That night, my beloved found out that he had been created for a specific purpose, and that God had an amazing plan for him. When the pastor asked if anyone wanted to ask Jesus to live in their hearts, Wayne left his seat and went forward to the altar. He fell to his knees and sobbed for joy as he repeated the sinner's prayer, and his life changed immediately.

He came home a completely changed man. At first, I joked that space aliens had kidnapped him, and I jokingly threatened to exercise my legal power of attorney. Time went by, and I realized this was not just a passing phase. He was a new man in Christ, and to be honest, he was an even more amazing man than before. The darkness and emptiness were gone—he was peaceful and content. Everything I had been trying to "fix" for all those years had been completely wiped away.

But still, I struggled with the changes in him. He was getting up early to pray and read the Bible, going to the new church twice a week, and even praying "victoriously" over me. He thanked God for his amazing Christian wife, and I wondered what he was talking about. I was utterly ashamed, and the only way I knew how to cope with the pain was to cover it up with scalding humor. But deep inside I was petrified, and I felt more alone than I had ever been in my life. At one point, I actually feared he would leave me for a "real" Christian woman.

This went on for almost a year. In sheer desperation, I methodically analyzed the Bible cover to cover. I traced Old Testament prophecy to New Testament fulfillment. I even read a weighty book about the history of the English translation of the Bible. It was all very intellectually compelling. But that was all it was. There was still no change in how I felt or acted.

At this point, Wayne was reading a series of books centered around the "Rapture" and the End Times. I indulged him and begrudgingly "scanned" through the books as fast as possible. Admittedly, I'm a book snob.

That's when September 11th, 2001 happened. There I was, working out on the Stairmaster, knowing my life looked like a fairy-tale on the outside, yet felt like a deteriorating mess on the inside. I was flipping through the channels to find something to take my mind off things when I landed on one of the news outlets. I was hit with instant horror: The World Trade Center in New York City, smoke belching out from behind one of the towers. Just a few years earlier, Wayne and I had attended a private business dinner on the top floor of one of the towers. I remembered how unsettling it was to look out of the windows and see planes close by, flying at a lower altitude. I continued to watch, assuming that the building could somehow be saved, when a huge commercial jet dove straight into the second tower.

*Planes are falling out of the sky.*

The blood drained out of my face and my chest began to tighten as I let both pedals of the Stairmaster slowly sink to the floor. A few moments later, live video was broadcast of a tremendous impact at the Pentagon.

*No…it couldn't be.*

Shortly after the coverage returned to the World Trade Center, the unthinkable happened. The second tower imploded, the floors pancaking together as they collapsed. The structure disappeared into a huge plume of smoke and debris. I still remember the screaming that could be heard coming from onlookers.

*It's the end. This is it. Just like in those books he made me read.*

What was happening that morning played out almost the same way as the plot of the first book, which describes the absolute chaos that descends on the entire world as the Rapture begins.

*Oh, dear God, if this is it, that means you've taken the real believers...*

*And I'm still HERE.*

The reality of that sunk in, and a wave of terror washed over me. My stomach twisted into knots and I struggled to get my breath.

*And if you've taken the believers...he'll be gone...oh God, no...*

If this was the Rapture, I had been abandoned in a world left to the Enemy while my beloved was already celebrating in heaven. The only way to know for sure was to see if he was gone. I gulped as much air as I could get into my lungs and took off running all the way across the house, down the stairs, and around the corner to his office.

*Please God, don't let it be too late, PLEASE let him still be there. God, I don't want to be left here alone.*

I got through the doorway and stopped, frozen in disbelief. He didn't have his television on, so he had no idea what had transpired over the last hour. I still remember the expression on his face as he looked up from his reading. It was a mixture of surprise and amusement at my absurd appearance that quickly turned to concern.

*YOU'RE HERE! YOU'RE HERE! And I haven't been abandoned!*

But no sound came out, just squeaking and wheezing noises from my lungs. I remember not being able to get any air, then my knees buckled, and I was headed to the floor. The next thing that I remember is him holding me up and asking me what happened, and if I was okay.

*NO, NO, NO. I'M NOT ALRIGHT. I THOUGHT YOU WERE GONE FOREVER.*

I was so overwhelmed I couldn't begin to explain what had happened.

*My God, what happened? Why would I be abandoned? How do I fix this?*

Imagine being judged guilty and sentenced to death, but you had no idea you had committed a crime.

You would think I would have gone straight to church the next Sunday and marched up to the altar to beg Jesus to forgive my sins, right? Well, that's not what happened. Even after that traumatic day, I still didn't understand how I would ever be able to change. I tried, but it was only superficial, and I was only able to keep up appearances for a few hours at best. This went on for another six long months. Wayne grew deeper in his faith, and not only tolerated me, but loved me even more. That just made me feel worse, because when I looked at him living in the peace, assurance, and joy I wanted so much, I hated him for it.

In March of 2002, I was three months pregnant. I had

to waddle on the treadmill for hours to ward off gestational diabetes, so I spent the time reading the Bible. I was an hour or so into my walk, looking for something that would justify a very unchristian opinion I had about a friend's marital situation. So, I read everything listed in the concordance that the Bible says about marriage. And it says a lot. And then suddenly, I had to stop the treadmill...

*Why does this always have to happen in the gym?*

The truth of God's Holy Word. I realized that I couldn't decide for myself which verses I wanted to believe and which I would rather ignore. I had to accept all of it or none of it. Could I trust God with all of my life or was I going to pick and choose what to surrender to him? Clearly everything I had been doing up until now was not working, and this Book was filled with stories of people like me who made terrible mistakes and were redeemed. Jesus promised his ways are higher and better than ours. "My yoke is easy..."

*Ok, but what about all the fun I have? I don't want to live a boring life dictated by a bunch of archaic rules.*

However, I wasn't really having fun watching my life deteriorate, even when I pretended I was. No amount of my own effort or the vast resources at my disposal could redeem everything that was going wrong. The Bible said all I needed was faith, and even that would be given to me. But I just wasn't sure I really believed everything in Scripture. It was a big leap for an engineer like me.

*Math. I'll calculate the probability that all those prophecies are coincidental.*

I did not even bother to finish the calculations after the probability passed a couple billion to one. I also remembered that I had seen a calculation of the date of the beginning of Jesus' ministry using the prophecy given to Daniel by the Angel of God. The prophecy, given hundreds of years before the birth of Christ, pointed to the exact year. A perfect, eternal, all-knowing God who spoke creation into existence, would bother to take away all the mess that I created? And wants to have a relationship with me?

*PLEASE! Please come into my life and take all this brokenness, give me a new heart, teach me, and lead me. And I will live out the rest of my days praising you and living my life in gratitude.*

That was it. The moment I asked him to live in my heart there was an immediate release, and I knew I was never going back. I called Wayne and the kids, my parents, and our friends. I told everyone what had happened and apologized for the awful things I had said and done to each of them. I told them from then on things would be different, and I would be living for him. I told the kids I wouldn't have all the answers, but there would always be a Bible left open on the kitchen counter so we could find them together. That next weekend, with all my family and friends in attendance, I waddled up to the altar of the church to kneel and ask Jesus to live in my heart and be my Lord and Savior. When I stood back up, I felt JOY!

After that day, I went through a season of immense learning from the new Christian friends in my life. I also started to notice how God was using me for his glory. The most memorable moments have been when the Lord has used the brokenness he redeemed in me to reach someone suffering with that same burden. I listened to the heart of a young college football player who truly believed that the sin he had committed was unforgivable. I had the joy of witnessing the Lord heal him of our shared sin, and that was the day I finally understood the true power of redemption. The Lord can use the worst thing in our life and turn it into a blessing.

My husband and I now have a relationship that is infinitely richer, because the depth of our love is based on the limitless love Christ has shown us. It has connected us in ways we had no idea even existed before.

During the last 18 years, we have endured some extremely difficult times, lost people we loved, faced illness, injury, and tragedy. His promise is not that we would have perfect lives, or that every prayer would be answered. The promise is he will be there with us, and for us, and he will somehow use whatever the Enemy inflicts on us for his glory. So, we continue to praise him regardless of our circumstance, sometimes even through our tears. We know he will always have the victory, and we will be delivered, no matter what. With that knowledge, we have endured what would have ended us before.

For my part, I am not alone in this world anymore. I have the joy of knowing the Author and Creator of the universe is always there with me, no matter what, and the closer I draw to him, the more blessings I receive. I have peace because I am not "in charge" of my life anymore; I gave that back to the only One who knows the highest and best way for me to live my life. I still have to battle the urge to keep certain things for myself or take them back from him, but I'm learning how much better things turn out when I leave them to him. I no longer allow the Enemy to hold me responsible for what is not mine to control.

I believe the greatest gift in salvation is the peace of knowing everything is right between me and my Father in heaven. And not because of how hard I had to work for it, but because of the sacrifice Jesus made on the cross. I may not have a "tranquil" life, but I do have peace in the most important part of my life:

*I have a Father in heaven, and he loves me enough to send his only Son to die on the cross, because that was the price that had to be paid to forgive my sins. Because Jesus has redeemed me, I can now be in relationship with my Father in heaven, and I will be there with him one day.*

I don't just believe this, I KNOW this. That is my peace, my assurance, my HOPE.

*Fonda and her husband have a deep heart for sharing the Good News of Jesus and actively support many non-profit organizations around the world. They have raised four children and have just welcomed their first grandchild.*

# LIVING OUT SURRENDER—
# RIGHT HERE, RIGHT NOW

SAVANNAH

What you just read in *My So-Called Fairy-Tale Life* was from my mom. It was her beautiful story of coming to a place of hope in Jesus. My story is a direct result of what the Lord did in her life.

When my parents came to the Lord, they were excited to bring their newfound faith into all aspects of our family life. They began by asking us children to attend church with them on Sunday mornings, but I wasn't too keen on the idea. Church was not exciting for me but I didn't want to let them down, so I went with them on occasion, but most of the time I made excuses for why I couldn't go.

The first time I truly met Jesus, I was 11 years old living in Ft. Lauderdale. The Palau team came to South Florida to launch a citywide evangelistic campaign they called Beach-Fest and my parents were excited to help organize a prelaunch meeting. The whole team came to our house for dinner and I attended as well. At one point during the dinner, the lead evangelist, Luis Palau, casually shared the Gospel with the group. It wasn't planned, and many of those in attendance were already followers of Jesus. He was just excited to share his heart with the group and remind them of the reason behind the campaign—to share the hope of Jesus with the city. I remember listening to him speak and hearing his passion for seeing people's lives change. Something in my heart started stirring that I had never experienced before. I ran up to Luis in front of the whole group and asked him if I could accept Jesus into my life and he prayed over me.

The only way I know to describe the feeling was like a breath of fresh air. I finally understood what all the excitement was about. Yet, being so young, I wasn't prepared for all the attacks ahead.

My parents decided to enroll me at a Christian school, and we were all excited about it. They provided me with the best resources, but I didn't thrive. It was as if others had planted seeds of faith in me, but I walked away and forgot to water them. *I didn't know I had to water them.* I thought becoming a Christian was a one-time event. Now I know differently. Becoming a Christian means working at a relationship with God, and yes, it actually takes work.

Over time I lost my way, but I still knew how to play the part to make everyone think I was a devoted Christian. I knew all the right verses and said all the right things, but there was no fruit in my life.

During my senior year of high school, I was still out on

my own path, apart from God, and making a lot of mistakes. When the time came to consider college, I earnestly wanted to follow my longtime boyfriend to the college he was attending, but my parents wouldn't allow it. They wanted me to attend Liberty University for a year, so they gave me an ultimatum: either I could pay my own way, or they would pay for a year at Liberty and then I could go wherever I pleased. Much to their pleasure, I went with the second option.

After a few months of attending Liberty, I made some really good friends. They were strong Christians who lived out what they believed. Knowing them caused me to look inward and realize that I had been faking a relationship with the Lord for too long. I wanted what these friends had—inward peace.

My friends and I attended Campus Community on Wednesday nights regularly. One particular night while I was there, I looked over at my best friend worshiping with her eyes closed and hands raised, singing out to God. In that moment, it dawned on me I had never experienced that before. I had never unashamedly praised the Lord. There she was, overwhelmed by the love of the Lord. I wanted to experience that same feeling. So, I spoke to the Lord.

"If all this is real…I want what they have, Lord."

It was simple, yet profound. Everything changed that night. I felt the Lord for the first time in a long time. It felt like he was wrapping me up in a warm hug and it all hit me at once—he's here. He's with me. He listens to me. He loves me…no matter what I've done.

I finally realized I was never alone because God was with me.

Soon after, I broke up with my boyfriend. It left me in a lonesome place. My friends were all happily dating, so I often found myself as the third wheel. Many nights it felt as though all I had was the Lord. But, his love proved to be more than enough. Over that year, I prayed for the man I would someday meet and marry. I prayed over his character, over his heart, I prayed he would love the Lord more than me and that he would lead our family.

At the end of my freshman year, I met that man at church. His name was Caleb. We got to know one another over the summer and he even asked my father for permission to date me. He was everything I had prayed for in a future husband and so much more. Right out of college we got married and moved to South Florida. We began working, traveled often, made friends, and even found a great church where we faithfully served together. One night, three years into our marriage, we were sitting on the couch and the whole house was silent. We looked at one another and realized something was missing, we wanted to expand our family. So we decided to start trying and just go for it. Having kids seemed simple enough, right?

I never considered things wouldn't work out.

Three months into trying, I still wasn't pregnant. I began to think, *something's not right*. I talked to my mentor who told me to stay calm and trust the Lord with this desire.

But I'm a type A person. I had a plan. And *this* was not part of my plan. I was determined to get pregnant. So we kept trying. In April of 2019, we finally got pregnant with our first child. I couldn't have been happier.

Six weeks into our pregnancy, my husband was asked to share a word during a series called "5 on 5" at our church. Five church leaders were selected to speak for five minutes and share a short sermon the Lord had given them. This was a huge opportunity for our family and we felt so honored. Caleb's parents even traveled down from Georgia just to be at the service. It was an exciting time, but it didn't stay that way.

I woke up that Sunday morning to blood. I thought it might have been implantation bleeding, so I tried to brush it off and get ready for church. On our way to church my stomach started cramping and I knew something wasn't right. My husband was so worried about me, but I didn't want to worry him without reason, so I told him to continue on and get ready to preach.

When we arrived at the church, I went to find my mentor and told her what was happening. With so much love and care in that moment, she told me the truth…I was miscarrying. I heard her words but I didn't want to believe them. I just denied it. A miscarriage wasn't in my plan and I wouldn't accept it.

I wanted to go home, and I almost did, but I couldn't bring myself to leave when my husband was about to preach. So, I walked into the service and sat in the back with a friend and cried as the realization that we had just lost our baby washed over me. My husband started preaching, and to my surprise his message was on surrender. My heart broke as I knew I was going to have to tell him what happened. We were going to have to live out surrender right here, right now. To surrender our lives completely to God, even the painful parts, even our baby.

Between the first and second service, I told him the horrible news. We had lost the baby. Caleb broke down in tears.

The second service started shortly after and he went back up to preach about surrender. Now it was personal. He was speaking about, and showing, what it looked like to have peace in the midst of pain…in the midst of surrender.

I knew deep down that if this was God's plan, then he had a plan for redemption as well. He wasn't going to leave me here in my pain. He was already writing the story of our future children. However, that didn't change the overwhelming grief and pain I felt in that moment.

Shortly after, we started trying to get pregnant again. After eight months, in January of 2020, we found out we were pregnant. It was our first baby's due date. With that, I was confident this baby was going to be it. This baby we would bring earth side! We told everyone, and excitedly prayed over our baby.

But a week and a half later, when I was five weeks along, we lost our second baby. I was devastated. I questioned God's goodness, his faithfulness, if he even had a plan. Yet through it all, my husband was a rock. He was there for me and constantly reminded me that we were not going to let the devil win. We were not going to give up hope.

During that time, I didn't want to see God's goodness, or feel his love, but he lavished it upon me nonetheless. I felt myself constantly drawn back to the Lord even when I wanted to distance myself from him. His love for me was so evident despite my pain and disappointment. Once again, the Lord was all I had and proved to be all I needed.

A week later, we went to see a specialist and get some answers. She advised us that it was in our best interest to stop trying for another baby. She asked me to get some bloodwork done at the local clinic so she could evaluate me further. COVID-19 was just beginning at this time so I chose not to make an appointment for the bloodwork to avoid the risk of possibly catching COVID at the clinic. I figured we would deal with it at a later time.

By February, we were in the midst of a really busy season in our lives. On Valentine's Day, my husband and I decided to make dinner plans and take time to reconnect. That night, God blessed us with our baby girl, Hannah.

The whole pregnancy was beautiful, even despite COVID-19. Every doctor's appointment was great. Hannah was always moving around and healthy. Her birth was beautiful, and she is such a blessing from the Lord. He knew the plans he had for us and for Hannah all along.

I'm here to tell you that God is so faithful! God was

faithful even when I wasn't. Even when I wanted to give up. Despite my reaction, God still blessed me.

Through every twist and turn life has thrown at me, I know God is still good. God will always be good. It's his goodness, faithfulness, and love that gave me hope in my darkest times. He offers the same hope to everyone, whether in dark times or not. He is ready to bring light to the darkness in which we find ourselves. We just have to surrender and trust him.

*Savannah and her husband live in South Florida and just welcomed their first child. God is currently teaching her about the joys and struggles of parenthood and becoming a positive role model for her daughter in the way that she serves, speaks, and cares for others. Becoming a mom has drawn her closer to the Lord as she recognizes her need for him daily.*

# NO HANDLE ON
# HIS SIDE OF THE DOOR

TIFFANY

When I think back on my life, I'm struck by the feeling my story is unique and yet common all at the same time. The facts of my story—my upbringing, my struggles, my challenges —are no doubt unique, and looking back, quite unusual. Yet, when I was in the midst of it all, I don't remember feeling unusual because, honestly, I didn't know it could be any different. As I gradually realized things could be different, or even better, I had an all-too-common human response—to climb into the driver's seat and take control. At least that's what I thought I was doing.

My parents divorced shortly after I was born. My mom left my dad for a man who was very handsome, but also very violent. My earliest memories are of my mom, late at night, screaming. I would often wake up in the morning only to be met by her bloodied and bruised face. It wasn't long until he beat a man to death in a bar fight and was sent to prison.

Now a single mother, my mom started tending bar at

night to make ends meet. When she would leave for work, she would put my brother and me to sleep in a coat closet with some blankets. It was her way of "keeping us safe" while she was at work. We knew it was morning when we saw the light coming in from under the door. There was no knob on our side of the door, so we would just wait for her to return home. She would typically return with two small cartons of milk and a small package of mini doughnuts for us to share.

I'm not sure when she started drinking, but she often slept through the day to "get ready for work." We moved often and the houses we lived in were rarely furnished or heated. I don't know that we knew anything was wrong. It was all we knew. Eventually, Child Services became aware of our situation and stepped in. I was seven years old when the state notified my dad of our situation. They said that if he did not claim us, we would be put into foster care.

My dad hired a man to escort us to Anchorage, Alaska, where he and his new wife were living. When we arrived, we were filthy, very thin, and "ate like animals" according to my dad. He made it very clear to us upon arrival that he had no interest in having kids, but that he "took his responsibilities seriously."

The first night in his home he made up a bed for us on the sofa bed in his guest room. In the morning, he found my brother and me snuggled up and asleep in blankets underneath the bed. He did not know we had never slept in a bed before.

I had always had my brother, so I don't ever remember feeling lonely, but the neglect and lack of nurturing had definitely taken its toll on me. I would have strong negative reactions to things and not know why. During the next few years, this lack of a loving foundation would provide fertile ground for feelings of being unwanted and unlovable to move in and take root.

By the age of 15, I was living on my own. My dad paid for an apartment and gave me a small amount of money for groceries. Because I never had a parent around, I was often invited to dinners at my friends' homes. This was my first real insight into how a normal family operated. The moms showed me how to make pie dough, iron my clothes, and set a table. I cherished this time and truly feel as though I was raised by the mothers of my friends. It was at this time I became keenly aware of how different I was. This is also when loneliness really set in and a lack of belonging began to open a deep sense of emptiness in me.

*What was wrong with me that I wasn't worthy of such love and community?*

This is about the time that I decided to jump into the driver's seat and really take control. I thought if I could fill the hole that was growing inside me with the things I believed were missing from my life, I could salvage this mess of a life I was living.

I stayed out of trouble, kept my grades up, and participated in sports and student government to stay busy. By this time, however, my brother was often in trouble and rarely went to class. He was the final person to leave. And when he was gone, I felt like I was truly left to travel this life alone. I tried to appear happy and unaffected by the life I was living, but inside I was deeply unhappy and very lonely. Yet I felt with absolute certainty, if I worked hard enough, a happy life was attainable.

By 18, my relationship with my dad was an occasional phone call and that was it. No holidays, birthday cards, or pats on the back. With the help of the high school counselors, my next move was college. It was a huge undertaking to move myself to the other side of the state, but the effort was worth it.

The furnished dorms and cooked meals in the cafeteria made college feel like a home, plus no one had family around. We were finally all in the same boat. It was a reprieve from constantly feeling different.

After I graduated, I moved to Portland, Oregon, and found my first job. I was on my way to building my dream life.

Eventually, I met a great guy and we were married. We worked hard and bought a small home. After four years, we had our son. Two years later, we had our daughter. Things were going really well. This is not to say I didn't feel ashamed of my upbringing or embarrassed because I didn't come from a good family. But with my hands firmly on the wheel, I just kept pressing ahead.

The big turning point came after we remodeled our dream home. I was so sure this would be the moment I would become happy and fulfilled. I walked through our new home, sat down, and cried. I felt exactly the same. I wasn't healed. On the outside, life looked great. But inside, I was still wracked with insecurities, questions of worthiness, and doubt I would ever be anything other than a deeply scarred, unwanted little girl.

It was about this time my friend asked me to join her for Bible study. I had never had any interest in church. That was where normal people went on Sundays with their families. I believed if anybody knew the truth about my past, they would never want me in their community. But, I was desperate. I needed to find a fix for my inability to find joy, or even, just maybe, contentment.

Persistence and dedication had gotten me a long way up to this point, so I decided to treat this Bible study in the same way. I went every week, read the Bible consistently, and did all my homework. For the next few years, I was a diligent student, but I still didn't really understand what all these Bible stories had to do with me. I heard words like "hope," "peace," and "loving Father." I listened to the stories about Jesus and how he loved broken people like me. But words in a book were not enough to pry my hands off the steering wheel.

One day I needed to pick up a prescription for my son at a little pharmacy downtown. I had both of my kids in the car with me and it was pouring down rain. At the last second, I decided to leave them in the car while I ran in to quickly grab the prescription. I don't really know why I did that. Thinking back, it was so far from anything I would ever normally consider.

As I entered the pharmacy, I noticed all the blinds

were closed. The next thing I knew, a man in a ski mask held a pistol to my head and told me to lie face down on the floor with the pharmacist and his assistant. When the gunman was done getting what he was looking for, he told us he was leaving but that we needed to stay down on the ground for eight minutes. If we tried to get up early, he would shoot us dead through the window.

The first thing I remember was thanking God my kids were in the car. The very next thing I remember were sun rays coming through the closed blinds. As I laid there on the cold floor, I felt a warmth and reassurance I had never felt. Somehow, I knew with absolute certainty that it was the Lord letting me know he was there with me. He was letting me know I was not alone.

I guess you could say that was my conversion moment. The point I realized God truly was who he said he was.

The Bible says to "trust in the Lord with all your heart and lean not on your own understanding; in all your ways submit to him, and he will make your paths straight" (Proverbs 3:5-6).

Gradually, over the next several months, the hollowness I felt growing up was replaced with an inner light. Jesus came to this world to love the unlovable. He doesn't ask for perfection or production. Once you believe the words in the Bible are written for you, you begin to know and understand the meaning of joy, peace, hope, and that it is possible for you to have them in your life. That was where I found myself.

I cannot explain how knowing I have a Father who loves me has changed me, but I know it has. This is not to say that my life doesn't continue to have hardships, but to know that I am loved and not alone has allowed me to let go of my armor and instead allow my fragile, tentative heart to receive and give love.

My husband used to ask me if I knew how hard it was to love an armadillo. My response to life had been to build a protective shield around me—to defend myself from getting hurt. Letting my guard down was a big ask, even from my loving husband. I had never really let myself be loved. It was too painful when that love left. And even more, I had never seen what giving love truly looked like—that it wasn't something to give or take away depending on the day or circumstances. It is so much more than that.

There is a famous picture of Jesus knocking on a vine-covered door. If you look closely, you notice there is no handle on his side. This is a visual I think of often. I now know God was always there. I just couldn't hear—or I ignored—his knocking. Once I opened the door, my life changed in ways I still don't understand, but I know God has plans for me and I trust him fully.

*Tiffany and her husband have been happily married for 29 years. They have two grown children and recently relocated to sunny Southern California where they are excited to be a shining example of God's grace and love.*

# SENSE OF PURPOSE

VALERIE

Jesus told his followers he came into this world so that we might have life and have it abundantly. I can certainly attest this has been true in my life.

As one who has made an effort to put Jesus Christ first for the past 30 years, my life has been a fantastic journey filled with family, friends, and God adventures. It has not been a life without pain and suffering, but it's been one where I feel a deep sense of belonging and mission, as well as an inner peace that has sustained me throughout the ups and downs that life invariably brings.

If you were to glance at my life today, you'd see a mid-life mother of four with a healthy marriage to a successful businessman. We live in a lovely neighborhood, I have many close friendships, and I live with a sense of purpose in my life. Were you to go back 50 years and look at my life as a child, neither you nor I would have been able to predict that I'd be where I am today.

I grew up in Marin County, California, just north of the Golden Gate Bridge. The youngest of three children, my parents divorced when I was two years old and I spent the majority of my childhood being raised by my mother. My mom was a lovely, caring person, but as a young single woman trying to raise three rambunctious children, she worked a lot and didn't have as much time to spend with her children as she'd like.

We never attended any type of church with my mother, in large part because of the family she was born into. She was raised by a single mom and never had a relationship with her father. In fact, she never really knew him, but it was believed that her father was a married deacon in an offshoot of the Mormon church. So, her experience of abandonment by a leader in a church left her with a sense that, if there was a God, he wasn't terribly interested in her.

I did not see my father very often as I was growing up. We would see him on holidays, occasional weekends, and on a family vacation or two each year. I knew he loved me, but he was busy with multiple jobs and his own single life. Trying to figure out how to help support us three kids was clearly a challenge.

It was with my father that I would attend church occasionally. He was raised Catholic and when I'd see him at Christmas, Easter, or Father's Day, he'd take me and my siblings to church. It was both exciting and a little strange. Exciting because it provided a little sense of religious identity in my life. Strange because I did not really understand why I was there, how to naturally participate, and I felt a bit like an outsider looking in. I thought that was my lot as a child from a broken home and I accepted it. There were pictures and statues of people, but church seemed more like a museum than something accessible and relevant to my current situation. If there was a God, he wasn't an active member in my life at the time, or so it seemed to me. However, I felt I had some sort of connection to God and religion through my father and his participation in the church.

I was a typical kid growing up. I enjoyed school, participated in sports, and was captain of the cheer team in high school. Like many teenagers, I sought acceptance from my peers and security in this world, striving for achievements and experiences.

My parents cheered on my pursuits of happiness and personal security. They longed for me to have the things in life that did not come easily for them with their struggles of being raised in relationally and economically poor families.

In spite of all my seemingly normal life experiences, I had this feeling inside that my life didn't really have much of a purpose. I was going through the motions but didn't know where my journey would take me. I thought it was all up to me and I'd do the best with the limited resources I had.

After high school, I went off to a college about 150 miles from my home. Far enough to force myself to separate from my childhood, yet close enough to come home on the weekends to see my family and friends.

There were two people in my life who were pushing me toward college. The first was my father, who never earned a bachelor's degree himself. He wanted me to be the best I could be and believed college would open many doors for me that he was never able to open for himself.

The second person who encouraged me to attend university was my sister Corinne. To me, she was about as close to perfect as one could be. Almost five years older than me, she was beautiful, charming, smart, playful, popular—it seemed she had it all and I tried to be like her in just about every way.

Corinne went off to college right after high school, the first in our extended family, so that's exactly what I aimed to do as well.

My college experience was fairly typical for an energetic, outgoing 80s girl. I took my studies seriously, but juggled a social party life with the other students. I was studying business and my hope was to be CEO of a company someday. After all, why not shoot for the top of the ladder?

It was in college that I took the time on a few occasions to attend the local Newman Center services (Newman Centers are Catholic campus ministry centers at secular universities). I had hoped to tap into my Catholic upbringing. I went looking for some sort of connection with God, if there was one, but I still felt like an outsider looking into someone else's religion.

I had heard that my sister Corinne had become involved in some sort of religion when she was in grad school, but I had no idea what it was about. Honestly, I felt like that might be something that would distance us as I did not have an initial interest, ability, or even curiosity.

During the summer before my senior year of college, I had the opportunity to visit my sister and stay the night with her in her apartment. The night before I went off to my summer job, Corinne sat me down at the foot of my bed to tell me something that had become very meaningful to her. With simple, penetrating words she said, "Sister, I need to tell you about Jesus." Honestly, that really caught me off guard as I thought Jesus was some sort of historical figure who had died centuries prior. I sort of put him in the "important founding people" category like George Washington. She went on to explain Jesus is real, alive, and wanted a relationship with me. That tugged at my heart, the sense of being wanted by someone close to God. I still had much to learn and understand. She explained how her life had changed once she put her faith in Jesus and how she deeply wanted the same for me.

She sent me off the next morning with a few small booklets that clearly illustrated the reason God had sent his son Jesus to live, die, and be resurrected. Jesus made a way for me to be in a relationship with God—a God who loved me, wanted the best for me, and who would be at my side every step of my life.

Corinne's excitement for Jesus, along with the new information I was processing, led me on a journey to explore who Jesus Christ was, who he is today, and ultimately brought me to a place where I decided to put my faith in him. I made that first step of believing in him and trusting that his plan for my life was the best for me.

It was quite remarkable the transformation that took place shortly thereafter. I no longer felt like the sole planner of my future and identity, like the one who had to do it all alone and hope for successful, happy outcomes. I began to meet with a new friend in an organization called CRU (known as Campus Crusade for Christ—an interdenominational Christian parachurch organization) who taught me about Jesus, introduced me to the Bible, and gave me answers for all the questions that came pouring out. It was such a relief—truly it felt like a new birth, an opportunity to start a part of my life I never even knew was an option for me.

My friendships and acquaintances that were not always the best influences began to be replaced by genuine, sincere friendships. My new friends were interested in seeing my understanding of Jesus continue to grow and desired that I would become strong and mature in my faith. We were on this journey together.

Life began to make a lot more sense. God had started to change my selfish, earthly pursuits into ones that were more focused on serving and caring for others. As my desires changed, so did my activities. And as my activities changed, so did my sense of peace and fulfillment.

Many years have passed since those early, formative years of first trusting Christ. I have been on an active journey of truly knowing Jesus and enjoying the plans he has for me.

While I have been far from perfect in trusting him each day, I've found that following him—and living my life as he would want me to—has led to a full life for me and those around me.

There are two key areas I have focused on which have helped me to stay in pursuit of his plans. The first is the Bible. I've found the more I study the Bible and get to know it, the more I understand the heartbeat of God and his guidance echoes in my mind. The second is simply surrounding myself with people who are in the same pursuit.

It is so fulfilling to experience the fruit God has grown through my life. I have a wonderful, healthy relationship with my husband who cares deeply for me and sets me up to be who God created me to be. I've raised my two biological kids into young adults who care deeply for others. I enjoy many beautiful friendships in my community and beyond. I've taken invitations to serve and support countless ministries. And, shortly after becoming empty nesters, my husband and I adopted two young foster girls from our community—two wonderful sisters who have brought so much joy to our family.

It has been my desire to be a light in my community and my family. One of my greatest passions is giving opportunities for friends and family to know and grow in a relationship with Jesus. This has included my single mom coming to know Jesus at 57 and being taken to heaven at just 65 with more peace than one could hope for. Since that time, my dad's faith has grown from one who grieved without hope to one who now lives in intimate, daily hope found in Jesus. What more could a daughter want? Well, I still seek more.

Many of the decisions I've made over my life were a direct result of the decision I made to trust Jesus while in college. There were countless times when, rather than reacting on my own impulses or chasing after a selfish desire, I sought what God would want from me and followed his path. The times when I've followed his lead have resulted in a sense of peace in my own life that have made a positive impact upon others. Often I say, "Wow, God, you have abundantly filled my life. Thank you. This has been more than enough." Yet God is not done using us on earth until he brings us to our home in heaven. Until that day, may he gain more and more glory through my life.

*Valerie and her husband have four children and live in Northern California. They are involved in many nonprofits serving people all around the world.*

# A LIFE IN THE SON

SALLY

I was an emotionally exhausted 24-year-old woman when I started therapy. For years, I had resisted the suggestions from family and friends to seek counseling. Yet here I was, finally, much to my own surprise, sitting in a psychologist's office and pouring out my heart. It was the beginning of a journey that would take me deep into the recesses of my memories. It would bring up past hurts, struggles, and pain. Things I had long forgotten. Things I thought I had escaped unscathed. It would also help bring about the most beautiful healing in my life.

It was there, in that psychologist's chair, when I realized for the first time just how much I was affected by my parents' divorce.

My parents divorced when I was 12 years old. I am the eldest of two children and after the divorce, we lived with our mother. She had a full-time job and virtually raised us single-handedly. Now that I am a parent myself, I see, as we say in Jamaica, she "used a basket to carry water." My mother was determined to care for us the best she could despite the circumstances.

I didn't have a close relationship with my father. I had very vivid memories of the disunity in their relationship before the divorce. And I always took my mother's side. After the divorce, I did not go to visit him willingly. At times, I flatly refused to go. I didn't realize it at the time, but I was very angry with him. He appeared to have moved on with his life and seemed happy we were not in the way.

As a young lady from a broken home, without the guidance, encouragement, or attention from my father, my self-esteem suffered greatly. I was his only daughter, yet I was not his prized princess. In fact, I was not sure what my worth as a woman should be at all. That feeling led me on an endless search for significance in all the wrong places. I explored a career in modeling and made poor choices in friendships. Not having the opportunity to attend university, I worked extra hard at my job to prove myself to others. Still, I was not satisfied. I felt empty and lost. And although I attended church on an almost weekly basis, I did not have an intimate relationship with my heavenly Father either.

On the advice of the psychologist, I wrote my father a very long letter. Not sure if I would ever deliver it, I started by telling him all the positive memories I had with him. I then shifted to talking about my disappointments. In the end, not quite sure what to expect in return but feeling the deep need to share my thoughts with him, I delivered the letter. To my surprise, he responded.

A few weeks later, he invited me to his home to talk. Another hard discussion. I wasn't sure I was ready, but I went anyway.

My father had read the letter carefully. He was very open with me. He answered my questions and gave me all the details I asked for. For the first time, I realized he had his own side to the story. He acknowledged he wasn't perfect. He had made many wrong decisions during the course of their marriage. He owned up to his share of hurts and also shared the ways he had been hurt. My father made himself vulnerable to me and shared his feeling of helplessness. It was the beginning of a very deep and profound healing that would come to our relationship, which I cherish to this day.

In the midst of this long road to healing, a close friend of mine from the world of modeling invited me to dinner at her house. She had recently gotten married and had something she wanted to share with me. I was expecting her to share about the joys of marriage, or maybe even an announcement she was pregnant. But, no. Instead, over dinner, she told me she had met Jesus.

Honestly, I can't remember all that she said. But I do remember how happy, peaceful, and content she seemed. And with all the sincerity and compassion in her heart, she invited me to her church where I could learn more about this man named Jesus. My simple response was, "Sure, one day."

After being in counseling for a few months, that day came. I called her up and told her I was ready to attend her church. And it was there that I was introduced in the most intimate of ways to the God who had chosen me—chosen me in him, from before the creation of the world, just as his Word says…

*"For he chose us in him before the creation of the world to be holy and blameless in his sight. In love he pre-destined us for adoption to sonship through Jesus Christ, in accordance with his pleasure and will—to the praise of his glo-rious grace, which he has freely given us in the One he loves"* (Ephesians 1:4-6).

I started reading the Bible for myself and realized there was a whole host of promises for me. I began to learn my worth. I began to understand my value, God's free gift of grace, and the hope of eternity. I learned how God loved me so much he gave his only Son—Jesus—to die on the cross for me. That's how valuable I am! The idea was almost too hard to believe. But I knew in my heart it was true.

After a year of regularly attending church and asking many questions, I was finally ready to fully surrender my life to God.

It started out much like any other Sunday, except I got to church a little bit late and ended up having to sit in a seat very near to the front. The message was entitled "Tentacles of the World." The pastor challenged each one of us to not leave the building the same as we had come in. We were challenged to surrender our lives with all our joy and sorrow to the One who was not of this world—to allow him to direct our paths.

As the service ended, I turned to leave. I was facing the back door and the next thing I knew, I was standing at the front of the church, facing the pastor. He simply asked how I was, and I broke down in tears. Poor fellow. My friend was at my side in an instant. She recounts that, being led by the Holy Spirit, I confessed my sins by name, asked for God's forgiveness, and prayed my way into the Kingdom of God! In obedience to God's Word, I was baptized the following week and have not looked back since.

There is a passage in the Bible that became a beacon for me after making this life-changing decision. It says, *"If that is how God clothes the grass of the field, which is here today and tomorrow is thrown into the fire, will he not much more clothe you—you of little faith? So do not worry, saying, 'What shall we eat?' or 'What shall we drink?' or 'What shall we wear?' For the pagans run after all these things, and your heavenly Father knows that you need them. But seek first his kingdom and his righteousness, and all these things will be given to you as well. Therefore do not worry about tomorrow, for tomorrow will worry about itself. Each day has enough trouble of its own"* (Matthew 6:30-34).

I wanted to trust in the Lord with my entire heart, leaning not on my own understanding of things, but submitting to God in all things. The book of Proverbs in the Bible says if I trust in the Lord with my whole heart, he will make my paths straight. I was ready for some straight paths!

As my relationship with my heavenly Father has grown, so has my relationship with my earthly father. He has been getting to know the adult me, and I am seeing him in a different light. I forgave him for not being there in my younger years. And my past experiences have allowed me to see the hand of the Lord even more clearly. Where humans fail…God never fails.

There is a godly man in the Bible named Jeremiah. He lived a difficult life, full of struggles and challenges. And just like him, I believe I have learned that no pain, disappointment, or challenge I have faced, or will face, will ever be in vain. It is all part of God's great plan that is still being fulfilled even now as I write this.

God says this in his Word: *"'For I know the plans I have for you,' declares the Lord, 'plans to prosper you and not to harm you, plans to give you hope and a future'"* (Jeremiah 29:11).

As I pursued God, I had no idea it would lead to healing in my relationship with my father. God's hand became more and more evident in my life. Even when I had not acknowledged him as Lord over all, he carried me through and has given me this opportunity to share my story with you.

Though it took many years, today my daddy and I also enjoy a close relationship. In October 2019, during the recent illness and subsequent passing of my stepmother (his wife of 30 years), he has allowed me into the deepest parts of his life.

We have grown to love and trust each other like never before. It breaks my heart to see him hurting. I want to help him adjust to this new chapter of life in any way that I can. Continuing on the efforts of my stepmother, I have been able to introduce him to our heavenly Father in very practical ways. In June 2020, I had the privilege of hearing my daddy confess that he, too, just like me and all the rest of us, is a sinner. I had the joy of hearing him ask Jesus to forgive his sins and give him the gift of eternal life in heaven. How exciting to watch him growing, even at the age of 76! He is reading Bible verses daily and the Holy Spirit is overturning life-long beliefs that were based on faulty teachings.

I'm now 48 years old. I'm married to a wonderful man and have three beautiful children. As we go through life in our home in Jamaica, God has given me the gift of healing and hope in my life where I hadn't even asked for it and didn't even realize I needed it. Each day, I see how the events of my past have shaped my present and this gives me deep, lasting, overwhelming hope for the future. And that hope reaches far beyond me. I see hope taking root in my family, my community, and in the people I come into contact with every single day—including many women whom I get to encourage as they walk their own road to healing.

*Sally lives in Kingston, Jamaica with her husband, Chris, and their three adult children. She participates in several women's Bible studies and she and her dad remain very close to this day.*

# I THOUGHT
# I WAS A CHRISTIAN

SUSIE

Before I met Jesus, I thought my life was fulfilled. I had the typical marks of a good life: comfort and prosperity, a loving husband, four wonderful children, and a life of volunteering and serving my community.

I felt my life was as good as it could be. But when you don't know the Lord, you truly don't know what you're missing. My life was seemingly full, but was empty of purpose.

And without realizing it, God was working on and pursuing me in a way I would only later come to understand.

Growing up, I thought I was a Christian. I was baptized as a baby and confirmed at school. But at the time, I cared more about the dress I was wearing than my spiritual condition.

And that's how my life was—I always believed in Jesus, but it was never life-changing for me. He was more of an accessory. And if I was honest with myself, I actually felt quite empty. I was reluctant to really dig in, look at myself, and address that reality.

Then came Easter. It was in the mid-1970s. I remember watching Franco Zeffirelli's "Jesus of Nazareth." It was an incredibly emotional experience for me. I didn't realize I would be so stirred on a spiritual level. Looking back, I see God was moving in my life then. He wasn't pushing himself, but he was giving me glimpses and a moment of recognition of who he really was.

The true moment of change in my life was the first Tuesday in May of 1978. I think back to that unforgettable day and am immensely thankful for it. It was that Tuesday I met Jesus personally and came to fully understand he is alive and active and moving in our midst.

Leading up to that memorable day, a friend had invited me to join a group of parliamentary wives who met in The Speaker's House of the House of Commons. I should explain that my husband, Timothy, was a Member of Parliament and had been for four years. I looked at the invitation, and without thinking too much about it, threw it away and decided I didn't need to go.

But God was already dropping thoughts into my mind.

A few days later, another invitation showed up in the mail. Somehow, looking at the second invitation, having thrown the first away, I decided maybe I did need to go. But first I needed a Bible. So off to the bookstore I went, looking for just the right one.

The bookstore was advertising the *Good News Bible* but I wanted the King James Version—the one I had been most familiar with at school. It was comforting to have that, but even still I remember, as I was walking down the hall to the room where the Bible study was, I felt like turning back. When I arrived, I was warmly greeted by a friendly American woman named Dottie. Later, I understood that she and her husband had dedicated their lives to help others in their spiritual life and growth through a ministry called Navigators (the Navigators is a worldwide Christian parachurch organization headquartered in Colorado Springs, Colorado; its purpose is the discipling of Christians with a particular emphasis on enabling them to share their faith with others).

I admitted to Dottie that I hadn't read from the Bible since I was in school, but regardless, she made me feel accepted.

We turned to John 15:5 in the Bible: "I am the vine; you are the branches. If you remain in me and I in you, you will bear much fruit; apart from me you can do nothing."

As I read that simple verse, it was truly as if Jesus was speaking directly to me. The words came out three-dimensionally. I understood that I was growing and there was a glow of warmth that filled me. My life was changed forever after understanding and believing that reality. Unfortunately, I was too British to say anything at the moment.

On going home, I thought to myself, "What's the right response?" Perhaps, I should put on sackcloth and ashes and throw my jewels out the window. But what would my husband, Timothy, say?

As soon as I got home, I read all of the Gospel of John.

And it was as if Jesus was sitting right there with me. I was especially impacted by the story of Nicodemus who questioned Jesus' teachings. Jesus clarifies with Nicodemus, in order to know God, he must be "born again." I immediately recognized this was what had happened to me at the Bible study only hours earlier.

I knew my heart was completely drawn toward the love of Jesus. I committed myself to Him, there and then, not even sure what that could possibly entail and not caring about the cost. This meant everything.

Even still, I initially found it difficult to share what had happened to me. When my husband asked about the evening, I simply said it was a very good meeting. It was the following week when we ladies met again, and there I shared with the group that it was the Word of God that impacted me. I couldn't deny what the Bible was saying directly to me. It was instantaneous to me, learning of God's love and me believing it. I never wanted to turn away.

When I realized Jesus was alive, I also realized my life—though filled with joyful activities and loving people—was actually quite empty. I needed this forgiveness and wanted to know what was written in the Bible, so meeting with Christians was important, especially to pray for our families and Parliament.

I was on the committees of several charities, planning events to help others…in other words, doing good works. I had a loving family but, ultimately, Jesus is the only one who can promise life "to the full" (John 10:10), or that "rivers of living water will flow from within" (John 7:38). The Bible tells us it would be foolish for me to "gain the whole world yet forfeit my soul" (Mark 8:36).

And Paul, proclaiming the truth of God, wrote: "But whatever were gains to me I now consider loss for the sake of Christ. What is more, I consider everything a loss because of the surpassing worth of knowing Christ Jesus my Lord, for whose sake I have lost all things" (Philippians 3:7-8).

I've lived an exciting and fulfilling life since that great day. Knowing Jesus, life is more satisfying, more meaningful, more purposeful, and fuller than anything I have or hope to possess. This knowledge saved my life. It continues to save my life to this very day.

Knowing Jesus and being with him is better than any life I could design or imagine for myself.

Yet even so, I find I need to remind myself of that reality in the busyness of life. It's so easy to grow distracted or to lose sight. With a large family of now 12 grandchildren, 2 great-grandchildren, and a life of responsibilities, I am so often pulled in different directions. There is a lack of constant commitment to my faith that I had hoped I would have when I first made the decision to follow Jesus all those years ago. What Jesus did for me on the Cross, shedding his blood, a sacrifice for me and all those who belong to and trust in him, is worthy of so much more devotion. But God is so kind. And his grace is enormous. It really is such Good News.

He is pursuing us always. He is pursuing you right now. If you even make the smallest step to listen to the Lord, he will meet you. His promise says, "Draw near to God and he will draw near to you" (James 4:8, ESV). God can change anybody—from politicians to prisoners—like he changed me. Jesus doesn't want anyone to perish, he is the God of hope, no matter who we are and what we've done. The challenge for me is to find ways I can best share the hope that is in me.

It has been an honor and a joy to serve together with evangelists like Luis and Pat Palau, their son Andrew and his wife Wendy, and fellow directors of the Luis Palau Association in the U.K. to support the work of the Gospel to all nations. In this fickle world that leaves one empty in the final accounting, what else truly matters?

*Susie and her husband, Tim, live in London, England. They are parents and grandparents to a large extended family.*

# WORK, EAT, RAVE, REPEAT

## ROWENA

My life before Christ looked full but was, in reality, quite empty.

As a child, I was loved by my two, high-achieving, hardworking parents. But in my soul, I knew something was missing. I searched for the missing piece in all the wrong places—mainly in inappropriate relationships with boys. Honestly, calling them relationships is generous. I was desperately searching for my identity in how loved I was by boys and people in general. If someone liked me, then I was happy. If they didn't, then I wasn't.

My vulnerability was easy to spot by predatory people. I was assaulted on the London Tube twice and genuinely, if there was a nutter within 500 miles, they would gravitate toward me.

A hedonistic party lifestyle seemed the answer. These were pre-Instagram days after all…but still the goal was to show the world how much fun we were having.

I kept the debilitating panic attacks to myself.

Things started to change for the better when I married Ron. He had always been my friend who also loved to party. We got married sometime later at a church (which is bizarre because neither of us had ever been to a church service—and neither had either of our families). I have never forgotten how kind the priest was to us. He didn't judge us. He just loved. He said, "This is your first step to knowing God. You may not take the next step for years to come but that is okay."

The first seed was planted, unbeknownst to us, by that loving man. When looking back on life, God has been with me always and, more than that, he has gone way ahead of me and was relentlessly pursuing a relationship with me, despite the fact that I didn't know him yet.

Up until that point, my beloved Ron was the only person in the world who really knew me and loved me just as I was.

He too felt the ache for something more in life. We started to talk about how there must be more to life than work, eat, rave, repeat. So, we started to look for an answer to the hole inside of us. We didn't know a single Christian—or anyone of any faith. You don't tend to find people like that at raves.

We looked in bookshops but found only more empty, man-made philosophies. What we were searching for was truth, we just didn't know what the Truth was or how to access it. There were also many "self-help" books—but all they did was point people back to worshipping at the altar of themselves (we were already very good at that).

We then decided to have a baby. Simple enough, millions of people do it. Why not us?

At the end of my pregnancy, at about 4 AM one morning, I was awoken by a sharp kick to my back and was shaking from head to toe. We went to the hospital and found I had a high fever. I was given many different drugs to help me and I had a major allergic reaction to one of the drugs. My body started to convulse, and doctors started to panic. I couldn't breathe or speak but I could see and hear everything. The doctor tried to get me to sign a consent form and I remember thinking, *What are you doing you silly woman? I can't breathe, let alone write!*

I was now in a coma.

They asked my poor husband who they should save— me or our unborn daughter? (That question haunted me for weeks afterward.) They then told him I wouldn't survive.

Our daughter was taken out quickly in an operation as her heart rate had dropped. I was being kept alive by a machine.

My mum and dad had started attending a church and when my husband rang them, they asked their church to pray. He also got down on his knees and said, "If you are there, God, now is the time to show up. I will do anything if you save my wife."

At that moment, when my family prayed, I opened my eyes. I was in Intensive Care in a room on my own, with my own individual specialist nurse and the blinds drawn. The nurse watching over me jumped as I spoke. My midwife was holding my hand crying.

Ron and our families were allowed in and they all were crying. I didn't—I was in deep shock, fear, and pain. The doctors kept coming in and trying to convince me it was a miracle. This was amazing because in the U.K., Christian doctors and nurses are not allowed to talk about Jesus or pray with patients. The doctors even tried to get me to repeat it. But I didn't. I didn't know what a miracle was. I had never been to church, read the Bible, or even met a Christian. So the word "miracle" meant nothing to me.

That ordeal began a horrific journey back to health—just me, Ron, and our beautiful baby, Isabella. We ran away and bought a bed and breakfast in Yorkshire, England. I think we were trying to get as far away as possible from the pain. But I soon realized we take pain with us, and now we were hundreds of miles away from family and friends. We clung to each other and our wonderful gift of a daughter who was a complete joy.

A few years later, we moved to Devon. One day, as we drove past a little store, Ron heard a voice say, *"You have to buy that place."* It was ridiculous, but Ron was convinced. So we rang the owners and asked if they would sell it to us. The owners gave us many reasons why they wouldn't do it. I then heard a voice whisper to me, *"Leave your number."* So I did.

People ask us if it was weird hearing a voice. But the weird thing was—*it wasn't weird.*

Someone rang us back 20 minutes later and asked how we knew they were thinking of selling. We told them we didn't.

God was placing us where we needed to be without us knowing.

We were very open with our customers about why we were there and how much pain we were still in some days. Straight away we noticed that some of them who befriended us were different. They had a light inside them that the rest of the world didn't have. We were uncontrollably drawn to them.

They showed us love and friendship but didn't seem to want anything from us. Being from London and working in advertising in the U.K. sometimes felt like I was swimming with sharks. There were times when it felt like people were only nice to me when I was useful to them. But these people were not like that.

They told us about Jesus. They actually say we bombarded them with questions. *Whatever.* They told us about Jesus.

One Sunday, we woke up and said we wanted to go to church, so we went. We spent the whole service in floods of tears with no idea what was going on in this small rural church by the sea. We described it like we had "come home." To what, we had no idea. But we knew we had "come home."

Those friends in the church taught us the Gospel—about Jesus and his love for us.

After a few weeks and an Alpha course, we decided to give it a go—this Christian thing—and we jumped in headfirst and said "yes" to Jesus. I will never forget Duncan, the Baptist minister, telling me, "Faith is not something you bolt on to your existing life, Rowena. It must become the center of your life and from which everything else flows."

It was the Truth. It was powerful, and it changed everything.

We were discipled and loved so well by that lovely little church. We started hosting a variety of things in the village and would tell anyone who would listen that Jesus loved them. We were on fire with his love. For 34 years no one had shared the Gospel with us. No one had invited us to church. We would actually say we had never met a Christian, which is of course a big lie! They just hadn't told us they were Christians.

Up until that point, it seemed as if we were not valuable enough to be told the Good News. We needed it. We searched for it, but no one shared it with us. So, if you are reading this and haven't heard yet—here it is, just for you, my darling….

Jesus loves you! He is relentlessly pursuing a relationship with you. You are not your circumstances. You are not what you have done or what has been done to you. You are a beautiful child of God and he is waiting for you with open arms. I wanted to tell you that in case you had never heard it. You see, I promised Jesus I would spend the rest of my life telling people how he loves them.

Four years after we left the village, my husband started training as a Church of England vicar. Me—the wife of a pastor! Are you joking, Lord? Have you not heard what comes out of my mouth?

But you see, Jesus doesn't look at our mistakes or

shortcomings. No. He sees you as you really are—a beautiful child of God. He is always there for you.

So, for those of us who are not paying attention, like me, God gets our attention in a more radical way. I love this description by theologian C.S. Lewis:

"Pain is God's megaphone to rouse a deaf world."

I was completely deaf. But in my deepest and most debilitating pain, God reached in and saved my life. Not just physically—that was the easy bit! He spiritually saved my life and took it from a temporary, plastic, meaningless life to an eternal one to be spent with him. What a gift! And I will be forever thankful that God used my pain for his good. And I will serve him for the rest of my days in thankfulness to him and our friends who took a leap of faith and shared his love with us.

You are valuable to him.

Dear friend, will you also accept the hope that is only found in Jesus?

*Rowena and her husband, Ron, live in Malibu, California where they currently pastor a church. They have been married for 22 years and have two children.*

# MY QUEST
# FOR THE ONE TRUE GOD

ADRIANA

I never personally engaged in the practice of lending my body to an evil spirit, but I knew many who did. Sitting in a quiet auditorium—red light flooding the room—a volunteer would step up to the platform. With arms waving rapidly above their head or palms slapping their thighs in quick succession, they would "free themselves" and make room for the evil spirits to enter their body. And when I say "evil," I mean "evil." The whole point of the exercise was to allow the bad spirit to experience the "good" of the borrowed body and consider their evil ways.

We, the audience, with the help of a medium, could ask questions of the spirit, talking to them as if in a normal conversation. And in the end—the goal of it all—would be to call the spirit to confess their wrongdoings, choose good, and leave their current hellish existence.

I knew from an early age it felt wrong.

Growing up in Buenos Aires, Argentina, I wasn't born

into this odd, uncomfortable world of Spiritism. My family was Roman Catholic. But at a young age, some close friends invited us to a special "spiritual" school. We were fully sucked in before we realized just how wrong it was.

As a family, we didn't talk much about our time at the school, which we had to pay to attend. We didn't practice any of the things we learned at home. In fact, we didn't practice much of anything at home. Yet this deeply spiritual and occultic experience shaped and guided me for many years, confusing me in the true ways of God.

My time as a child in this school quickly became less of a spiritual journey and more of a spiritual search. I came to this school not because of my own desires, but because of my parents' prompting. Yet the longer I was there and the older I became, the list of questions only seemed to grow. And never did I find answers within the walls of that school. As I would sit in these practices, sometimes two to three times per week, as individuals opened themselves up to spirits, I would be flooded by profound, existential questions…

*Who am I?*
*Where did I come from?*
*Where am I going?*
*What's the purpose of my life?*

They were the questions so many of us wrestle with. And with no real answers, I was left with a deep sense of emptiness and despair.

My questioning was not because I was unhappy. I genuinely had a very happy childhood. My dad was a doctor. My mom was a teacher. We had everything we needed. But this school, which purposed to have the deep answers to life, had no answers for me whatsoever.

It all came to a head one day when the "spiritual leader" of the school ran off to Europe with most of the school's funds. It was the last thing I needed to realize I should no longer be part of this group. They had completely broken my trust and had never offered me anything of value.

Though I put an end to my dark spiritual practices, my parents and my sister continued on in the school. My family would often ask me why I stopped attending the school. I would simply say I was looking for something else. (My parents always allowed and welcomed us to be free in making our own choices.) As such, they didn't have a problem with my conversion out of Spiritism.

And that's when my real quest for the one true God began to take off.

For so long, I was convinced I was walking the right path. I didn't have the answers I was seeking, especially as they related to God, but I was doing all my leaders were telling me to do, obeying my parents, and doing well in school. Yet a voice in my head kept nagging at me. In the quiet of the night, it would say to me, "If God is real, your life needs to change." I heard these words in my soul for several months.

In college, my anatomy teacher sensed my searching. He gave me a Bible and quoted Jesus in Luke 11:23: "Whoever is not with me is against me, and whoever does not gather with me scatters." It hit me to my core. He was right. I felt lost, scattered, and alone. I was a person who was seeking rest but could not find it. I knew I was not on Jesus' side, because there is no gray area with him. You are either black or white. I understood I was on the opposite side of what the Bible teaches about Jesus, the Lord and Savior.

This verse made such an impact on my heart and brought to light another question: Would I be with God or against him?

When we broke for summer, I went on vacation with my family and took my Bible with me, reading it passionately. I specifically remember reading the resurrection story of Jesus. No one had ever told me that Jesus was alive, that he was the true God who overcame death, and that he grants eternal life to everyone who trusts him. For the first time, I read the Gospels, Psalms, and Proverbs, and my heart overflowed with hope and joy.

When I saw my anatomy teacher the next fall, I told him all that had happened and I asked him many questions. I had so many doubts about so many things. He encouraged me to attend an upcoming event to hear a man speak about Jesus. And when I went, I was blown away by his words. The God he was preaching about was far more real than the one I had previously known.

It was the following Easter when I was invited to a church service by a friend where I finally gave my life to Jesus. In that moment, my life changed completely and forever. It's hard to put the experience in words, but the wonderful feeling of fulfillment filled my heart. I knew for sure that the existential emptiness I had experienced for many years had now gone. My search was over.

It was a progressive change, from the inside out. Step by step, day after day, I was being renewed. From my inner thoughts, feelings, and beliefs to my way of speaking and relating to people, I was truly becoming a changed woman.

It wasn't just a religious change either, but a change that impacted every part of my life. To my surprise, God had already started to work in me even before I ever accepted him. I then realized it was the Holy Spirit who had been at work in me for many years. He was the one prompting the questions, planting the seeds of doubt about my previous beliefs. He shattered many mental schemes I had that were contrary to the abundant and healthy life God has in mind for all of us.

One by one, God showed me the truth through his Word. For example, I believed in reincarnation. But when I read in Hebrews 9:27 that every human will die and ultimately face judgment, that belief I had held on to for so many years simply vanished. From then on, I started to value every action and thought, because I realized I only had this one life which would be judged according to my actions.

Slowly, nearly daily, God continued to strip away my

old thinking and habits, teaching me a new way of life. He taught me that my body was a temple of the Holy Spirit, that I am sacred, and that I have value. He taught me how my flesh—that innate inner-self that was always leading me in the wrong way—had died. It had been crucified with Christ, and now he lives in me.

It was wild and new and different and exciting. And deep down, I knew it was right. I knew that the real secret for a good life was letting Christ live more and more in me each day.

And so, with God's help, I put down my pride, my anger, and my rebellion. I laid them at his feet so he could take them out of me. And little by little, God started to transform me, and he continues to do so each day because his work in me is not finished.

I was the first in my family to choose Jesus, but I never stopped praying for them and took every opportunity to tell them about the life-changing love of God. Eventually, they, too, made a commitment to follow Jesus!

Today, I am happily married. We recently celebrated 45 years of marriage. We have four children who are all believers, married, and serving the Lord in different ways. By God's grace, we also have five granddaughters and four grandsons (one in heaven).

I want to thank God with all my heart and give him all the glory for rescuing me from hell and making me his daughter. I want to thank him for fulfilling the promise the Bible makes in the book of Acts when it says, "Believe in the Lord

Jesus, and you will be saved—you and your household" (Acts 16:31). That has been my story. And I pray it is yours as well.

Now that I have experienced the new life in Christ, I can see all the lies and deceitful words that were behind the practices of the Spiritism I grew up in. People who practice Spiritism are on a search for God but they are looking in all the wrong places. They are confused and trapped in a practice that will never fulfill them. It will never give them the answer or purpose they so desire. The hope they are searching for can only be found in Jesus. He changes our hearts and our lives. Spirits do not and cannot change us. Spiritism will only ever give momentary solutions or glimpses of the greater spiritual world, but only in Christ will your emptiness be filled permanently with love, peace, grace, and so much hope.

Do you need this peace today? It can be yours. All you have to do is ask.

*Adriana and her husband, Ruben, live in Buenos Aires, Argentina. They have four children and nine grandchildren. As a couple, they have been actively involved in serving God throughout Latin America for more than 40 years.*

# THINGS ONLY GOD
# COULD MEND

TANGIE

"One of your babies is dead and the other one is in distress!" Everything was happening so fast. The nurse threw back my hospital sheet, adjusted my gown, and started prepping me for an emergency C-section. In March, I was a happy-go-lucky junior in high school with hardly a care in the world. And now, eight months later, I was giving birth to twins!

I never intended to become a single, teen mom. Yet, there I was, heading into my senior year carrying not just one baby, but two. Tory was my high school sweetheart. We had grown up together and hit every milestone together. He was charming and thoughtful, funny, and an all-star athlete. But, nothing could prepare us for the story God had for us.

My entire pregnancy was plagued with sickness. At 17, my young body was not prepared for the strain of carrying two babies. And from the beginning, I experienced nausea, excessive vomiting, and fatigue. As time went on, my blood pressure began to rise, my heart rate increased, and I developed an insatiable thirst for water. My health continued to spiral with every passing month and on Sunday, October 29th, I began to feel worse. I developed a fever and felt a general malaise. My mom called my doctor and told him my symptoms. His instructions were for me to continue taking medication he had prescribed previously and to just keep my appointment for the upcoming Thursday. By Thursday, November 2nd, the day our twins were born, I was 30 weeks pregnant and my health had completely deteriorated. I had lost 20 pounds in six days. I was diagnosed with preeclampsia, suffered a stroke in my pituitary, and developed gestational diabetes insipidus, which explained my excessive thirst. I was literally at death's door by the time I arrived at the hospital. Several of my organs had started to fail, so my doctor rushed me into the operating room where I gave birth to my precious and tiny son and daughter. I felt sad and confused and angry. And God felt far away. Where was he and why was this happening?

Tory was right by my side for the birth of our twins. Our little girl, Torian, had serious complications and was whisked away immediately. Our sweet boy, Tory Jr., was lifeless. A doctor later told us that he had likely died two or three days prior to delivery. We were heartbroken. How had this happened? Why did this happen? Why would God allow me to carry twins knowing only one would survive? Too many questions and not nearly enough answers. God was not providing any answers or comfort. I felt betrayed and abandoned.

In the hours following delivery, my health continued

to decline. The next day, Friday, November 3, 1995, I was transported via ambulance to Vanderbilt University Medical Center. Upon entering the E.R., the doctor in charge of my care informed my mom I was very sick and I would likely not live through the night. I was in a medically induced coma for a few days and my prognosis was grim. Even if I survived, it was very likely I would either need medication for the rest of my life or I would need a kidney transplant.

Then on November 6, my 18th birthday, doctors told my family that all the treatments had worked, and it looked as though I would pull through. My preeclampsia was followed by a very rare condition known as HELLP syndrome. Knowing what I know now, it was a miracle I survived. After 11 days in the hospital, I was finally discharged to go home—but with no babies and no answers. I felt empty—empty of joy, empty of hope, and empty of wonder. And God was still silent.

My son's funeral was held on Tuesday, November 7, 1995. I was still in the hospital and unable to attend. Heartbroken, angry, and confused I lay in my hospital bed trying to make sense of it all. But none of it made sense. In hindsight, I did everything my doctor said. I never missed an appointment and I called him every time I had questions or if something seemed amiss. Yet, there I was, mourning a son I would never hold or see again this side of heaven. I am thankful Tory was able to attend the funeral. He described our son's sweet little face and what he was wearing as best he could. He gave me as many details as he could even though he himself barely had any time with our son.

"His coffin was so small; it was white and light blue and oval-shaped. He was wearing a thin, white, christening gown and his thick, black hair lay smooth across his head." It was as if he was just asleep. But, he wasn't. He would never open his eyes or smile, never grow up with his twin sister, never have a favorite football team or a favorite color. There are so many memories and milestones that would never come to be.

As the days went on, I grew increasingly angry. Angry my doctor didn't listen to me. Angry I didn't just go to the Emergency Room when I knew something wasn't right. Angry I trusted my doctor. Angry my son was dead. And most of all, angry that God allowed it all. "God, talk to me! Tell me it's not my fault. Tell me it is my fault. Just tell me something!" When I think back to that gray November day, my heart breaks for the four children in that operating room. Shattered and broken. The four instantly became three. I felt punished and rejected. And God felt like a harsh judge allowing me to be crushed under the weight of my choices, my sins.

For many years, I wondered why. Why did my son have to die? Why did he allow me to get pregnant with twins when he knew I wouldn't leave the hospital with both of my babies? Why take Torian's twin brother—her built-in best friend? I never got an answer to those whys. Instead, the closer I grew to him and the more I read his Word, my questions started to change. What do you want me to know about your character? How do I apply that knowledge in my life? And how do you want me to use my testimony to point others to you? Yes, at times I would find myself still wondering why. But those questions no longer consumed me. As an adult, I realize there are so many questions I will never have answers to on this side of heaven. However, questions like these cause me to seek him and tell others about the Father that has loved me and carried me through the hardest days of my life.

Nearly seven months after the twins were born, Tory and I graduated from high school. A week after that, Tory broke up with me. I was crushed. He left for college several weeks later and I was left to raise our daughter without him. I had to figure out how to provide for her. How to further my education. How to set Torian up for success, even though all the odds were stacked against her. In 1998, I moved out of my parents' home and into public housing—also known as the Projects. I was a teenage mom on Medicaid, food stamps, and WIC (Women, Infants, and Children). I never imagined I would find myself in this situation, struggling to make ends meet. Yet, there I was. Me and Torian. Moving out on my own was empowering and I was ready to make my own decisions, decisions that would place me and Torian on a path to better things. Eager and optimistic, I no longer felt estranged from God.

God was pursuing me, not that he hadn't been before. But now I was aware, no longer solely focused on my losses, but also on his gifts and goodness. For a couple years after having Torian, I was a part of a Bible study for teen moms. The women leading the group had been my spiritual mentors prior to me getting pregnant. So, it was only natural to continue life with them and to introduce my daughter to them. Between those ladies, family (mine and Tory's), and friends (some who were also young moms), our lives started to take shape. We developed a routine and I had goals for Torian and myself. And most of those plans included Tory.

I worked part-time in retail and started school at the local community college. The years were long and hard and short and fun. In May 2000, I graduated with an associate degree in Mass Communication. And that fall, my sweet little Torian started Pre-K at New Hope Academy. Torian and I were growing up and learning together. My shy preemie had overcome so many obstacles all before turning four and I was incredibly proud of her.

The following spring, Tory graduated with a bachelor's degree in Management Information Systems and moved back home. It was all coming together, or so it seemed. We were more mature. We both finished school and I had held it together while he was away at school. While Tory wasn't ready to commit to me, he was committed to being a loving and present father to his daughter. In many ways, we looked like a loving, intact family. But that's not at all what we were. There was still a spark between us, that much was true. However, Tory's time away from me hadn't made his heart grow fonder.

We "dated" some over that summer. Tory looking to strengthen our friendship and me looking to convince him that I was the one for him. One night after a party, Tory and I hooked up and it felt as though things were changing. But in reality, that was not the case. I was hoping for more and Tory was content with where things were. A month later, I found out I was pregnant. I told Tory and he was furious. He immediately felt trapped, thinking I had gotten pregnant intentionally. Nothing could've been further from the truth. Tory didn't believe me, and he immediately withdrew from me.

Here I was again, unmarried and pregnant. The seams of my short-lived successes were starting to unravel. I had just enrolled at one of our state schools to work on my bachelor's degree. With that enrollment came a full tuition scholarship and an unwanted pregnancy. I began to consider abortion. I did not want to go through another potentially hard pregnancy with a man who didn't trust me. My heart was breaking. How could I even consider killing my baby after losing one? Why would I choose to put myself through that again? And what about the baby? What type of life would they have, born to feuding parents and into poverty? I would tell myself there isn't even a heartbeat, yet. I would go from trying to convince myself that I wouldn't actually be taking a life to how in the world could I ever consider taking away a life after having already buried a child.

I took additional pregnancy tests hoping the previous ones had been false positives. They weren't. I was pregnant. I told Tory I was considering an abortion and he was okay with it. He stressed that it was my decision, but he did think it was the better choice for our situation. So, we went to Planned

Parenthood for a consultation and we made an appointment to come back for the abortion procedure. I probably cried every day from the time I found out I was pregnant until the day of the procedure. The procedure that never happened. I couldn't do it. I could not end the life growing inside me. I called Tory the night before and told him I was keeping the baby and I understood if he didn't want to be involved. Although he believed not having another child made sense, he, too, had reservations about ending a life. So, there we were. Moving forward with a pregnancy we were not prepared for and in a relationship that was nonexistent.

My second pregnancy proved to be difficult as well. I had morning sickness throughout, along with fatigue, and a very broken heart. Tory went to almost every appointment and we even heard our baby's heartbeat for the first time together. In December 2001, we found out we were having another baby girl. Just writing this makes me smile. I had no idea what plans God had in store for us.

By now, I was confident in my decision not to abort and was making room for a second child in my home and my heart. By early April, I had developed complications in my pregnancy. I was hospitalized for a week after developing pancreatitis. I eventually recovered, but three weeks later I had developed pancreatitis for a second time. This time, my obstetrician decided that delivering my baby girl would be the best option for both of us.

On Friday, May 3, 2002, 15 days before her due date,

I gave birth to my third child, Tariah. I had a second C-section and Tory was right by my side. When the doctor pulled Tariah out, there was no cry. Nothing. The umbilical cord was wrapped around her neck a couple of times. After clearing her airway, the nurse handed me my beautiful baby girl. She never cried. She just stared at us with her bright eyes. She was really here; another precious life was in my arms.

After eight days in the hospital, I left with my baby girl. Tory continued to provide for his daughters. It was obvious how much he loved them. We took care of our daughters, but we lived separate lives. Things were hard after we were released from the hospital. I had developed pneumonia and severe anemia. I was re-admitted and Tory cared for both girls, with the help of his older sister, while I struggled to recover. Once I was released to go home for good, I developed a new normal. Torian started first grade, while Tariah and I developed our new mother/daughter rhythm. All seemed normal until Tariah was four months old. She seemed agitated at times and began developing ear infections along with fevers. This persisted for months, worsening around eight or nine months old. Her pediatrician wasn't worried about her chronic ear infections, along with fevers. I, on the other hand, believed there was more going on.

A couple of months after her first birthday, the pediatrician was concerned that Tariah had not grown since her last check-up, had persistent fevers, and chronic ear infections. She wanted a better idea of what was going on. In late July, lab work indicated that Tariah needed to be hospitalized to have better conclusive tests run. In the end, we spent two weeks at Vanderbilt Medical Center.

While there, the doctors discovered spots on Tariah's liver. After a biopsy, the diagnosis was Langerhans Cell Histiocytosis (LCH), commonly referred to as histiocytosis. We had never heard of this rare childhood disease. So rare, only 1 in 200,000 children are diagnosed with this disease annually. Research goes back and forth regarding whether or not LCH is a type of cancer or a type of autoimmune disease. In recent years, research indicates that LCH is classified as a cancer. After this diagnosis, doctors spent time preparing us for what treatment would consist of. Tariah was considered a high-risk patient due to a systemic disease and her age (under two). Her classification as systemic is due to having liver, skin, G.I. tract, and lymph node involvement. In short, our baby girl was incredibly sick with a life-threatening disease that we had never heard of.

In August of 2003, a port was placed in Tariah's chest to allow for an efficient delivery of chemotherapy and to draw blood. We were looking at a minimum of two years of chemo, appointments, and scans. Our worlds were rocked. Our family and friends joined us in praying for her complete healing. As much as Tory wanted to pray for our daughter, he felt he wasn't worthy of asking God to heal Tariah. So, his initial prayer was for God to "get him right" so he would feel qualified to pray for his family. Tory decided to start attending church and he began a Bible study where our friend, Chris, was the pastor of the church. Unbeknownst to us, Pastor Chris had spent years praying for both Tory and me. He was rejoicing that God had answered his prayers. Glory!

A year into Tariah's chemotherapy, her disease progressed—spreading to her pituitary. This was unexpected and disheartening. We started a third type of chemotherapy hoping to kill the disease. As a result of LCH now affecting her brain, Tariah developed diabetes insipidus. Our sweet girl continued to fight and have joy despite everything she was enduring. The irony was not lost on us. Here we were praying for the very child we had planned to abort; praying that she would live.

After 26 months of chemotherapy, Tariah was in the clear, given the badge of honor: NAD. No active disease. We returned for regular scans, blood draws, and follow up appointments for an additional eight years. To date, Tariah continues to have endocrinologist appointments and Cancer Survivorship Clinic appointments. With all the chemotherapy she received at such a young age, Tariah has had no neurocognitive side effects. God is good and has been so gracious to our family.

Through all this, Tory was beginning to know the Lord for himself. His eyes were opened, and his heart softened. Tory often says that Tariah's life turned him to Jesus. His love for her and his desire for her healing led him to the cross in a way he had never experienced. I realized that through all the hardships, I had made Tory an idol. It had never occurred to me how misplaced my worship was. I was looking to him to "fix" all my problems. I had placed unrealistic expectations on him. Expectations that could only be met by my God. I realized God was the one who met all of my needs and only he was worthy of my worship.

On Saturday, December 1, 2007, Tory and I were married. We stood before God, family, and friends and promised to love each other for better or worse, 'til death do us part. It's been said that our love story had a fairy-tale ending. It is a beautiful story of redemption, but the story isn't just about us. It's about the One who loved us in spite of ourselves, despite our sinful nature, despite our wickedness and, at times, blatant disregard of his Word. That's the love story. He is love and his love is never-ending.

For years, I only saw myself as a bystander in God's story, watching how he weaves parts of history to present day. I'd watched him protect and redeem others in his story. Never realizing he was doing the same with me. I'm just as much a part of his story as Moses or King David or Judas. He sees me just as he saw them, as much as he sees you. And as sweet and redemptive as our love story is, it pales in comparison to God's redemptive love for us.

*Tangie, her husband, and two daughters live in Tennessee. Tariah is in her freshmen year at Vanderbilt University.*

# AIN'T NOBODY
# LOVES ME BETTER

EMMA

Let's talk about *love.*

Psychologists tell us that as humans, we need to know we are loved, accepted, and valued in order to live a balanced life. Now let's talk about music for a moment, the universal language—it moves us to tears, reaches emotions we never knew we had, and can sometimes be our saving grace, especially during tough times.

If we go way back to the 60s, The Beatles told us, "All you need is *love.*" But it's not just the Beatles who have been telling us that through the centuries. Back in the 90s and the 2000s, it was rumored that 90 percent of songs were *all about love!* Romance, candle-lit dinners. The era started with the likes of Luther Vandross and Mariah Carey singing "Endless Love." Throw in "Crazy in Love," by Beyoncé and Jay-Z, or "Where Is the Love?" by Black Eyed Peas. It is estimated there are now around 100 million love songs in the world today. We seem to be obsessed with LOVE!

What does this have to do with my story of hope? Well, I grew up in Essex, East of London in the U.K., with my family. Everything seemed perfect in the sense that both my parents were together, had jobs, and would take my sister and me to church each week. However, one thing was missing. My dad *never* told me he loved me. I'm sure some people will read this and think "get over it" or "you should hear my story—that's nothing!" But as a young girl, I wanted to know and hear those three words from my dad. I wanted him to be proud of me; I desired for him to say, "Hey Emma, what shall we do? Go bowling? Get ice cream at Mackie's?" He just wasn't that kind of dad.

I remember one day being out with my dad and older sister, and—for some reason—right in front of me, he said to my sister, "Sara, you're my favorite daughter." Hello! I'm standing right here! I wanted to shout in his face. Did that mean if she was his favorite then I was his least favorite?

I decided I would take matters into my own hands. Like so many others, I decided to find the love that was missing in my life by finding myself a boyfriend. If I could find a guy who would say, "I love you," my world would be complete…we would get married, have a goldfish and a guinea pig, and I would be happy forever after. Sadly, it didn't work like that. Most of the guys I dated didn't know what real love was, and those who did say those three words didn't mean them—oh no…they used those powerful three little words to get something else. I'm sure you can guess what that was! (I'm talking more than a snog behind the bike shed!)

As I said, I had been brought up going to church and I was taught to wait until I was married to have sex. So when a relationship got to a certain place and the guy wanted to go further, I would explain I wanted to wait. Do you think they waited? Of course not! They had their sneakers on, and they ran away as quickly as possible. There were plenty of other girls in Essex that would go the full way, so why wait for me? There's little old me looking for love, acceptance, and value, yet being dumped and rejected by every boy who came my way.

Then, along came Neil. I had left school, got myself a job working for the Queen's bank, Coutts & Co., and this amazing guy started taking me out. He told me he loved me and to top it all, he was a funny guy. Come on, we all like to have a laugh, don't we? Makes us feel good, doesn't it?

The day came when he wanted to take things further, and this time it was different. I didn't want to get rejected. My heart couldn't take it and I didn't want to lose him. Maybe I was asking too much? Maybe waiting was old fashioned and the Bible was out of date?

I made a decision not to get hurt again and had sex with him.

A couple of months later Neil called me at the office to say he had to cancel our date that night, so I was like, "Okay, shall we get together tomorrow?" But he was acting strange and said he couldn't, so I asked him when we should reschedule. That's when he told me, "Emma, I don't want to see you again."

I just didn't get it! Everything was okay, wasn't it? So, I asked that fatal question: "Why? Why don't you want to go out with me?"

His response hit me hard...

"*Fat* women don't do anything for me."

With that one sentence, my self-esteem crashed. If he thought I was fat, then that meant I was ugly, unlovable...I would never find true love. I had given him everything—even my virginity—and he threw it back in my face. I felt worthless. I had two choices: brush it off and not believe it or change the way I looked. Sadly, that day I made a mistake as I chose the latter.

I started hitting the gym for two hours every night thinking I could lose weight and tone up. Have you ever been to the gym? It's flipping hard work and my body wasn't changing quickly enough. So, I decided to skip some meals. But I had another problem...I love my food! Do you love your food? I wasn't willing to sacrifice this. So, "Plan C" had to be created. I decided to eat all the food I love really quickly and soon after I would make myself sick. I could enjoy the food without putting on any calories. This was great! I was in full control, or so I thought.

Two years down the road, I was in a very dark place, lying to myself and everyone else. My relationships were damaged because I had an eating disorder called bulimia, making myself sick up to five times a day. They call it the secret illness because you simply lie and don't admit it to anyone. I remember one night sitting on my bed asking myself the question: "What happened?" I had stopped going to church a long time ago and felt too guilty to talk to God. I was all alone.

I started to reminisce. I remembered how my mum took me to the QPR football stadium when I was just 12 years old to hear an evangelist—Luis Palau—share the amazing Gospel that brought me into a relationship with my heavenly Dad…God. He told me God loved, valued, and accepted me just the way I was. That was the most amazing day of my life when I truly understood that I, Emma, could have a friendship with the Creator of this world, a God who was alive and kicking and active still today. In the past, I had religion, but now I had a relationship. I used to love talking to God and going to church. What had gone wrong?

Maybe I was too young coming to faith, I hadn't really lived yet? Maybe the world had swallowed me up? There are so many pressures to look, act, and be a certain way to fit in today.

But all those years later, I remembered that feeling I had when Luis spoke to the stadium full of people, young and old, way back in 1984. It felt like I was the only one standing there; it was as though Jesus was using Luis' eyes, voice, and hands. As Luis pointed to the crowd, it appeared his finger was directed at me! Jesus was speaking to the 12-year-old girl then, and he was speaking to the 19-year-old girl now.

I knew I needed to come home.

I don't believe there is a formula; however, I do believe what I did that night changed my life forever:

I said sorry. "God I'm sorry for not trusting you, not believing your love was enough for me. Sorry I'm damaging this awesome body you've given me, this precious, beautiful body. Will you forgive me?" The Bible promises us forgiveness: "As far as the east is from the west, so far does he remove our transgressions from us" (Psalm 103:12, ESV).

I accepted his forgiveness. This can sometimes take time but it's so important we accept his forgiveness…and forgive ourselves.

I chose God's way. I knew I wasn't living life in all its fullness as promised by Jesus: "The thief comes only to steal and kill and destroy; I have come that they may have life, and have it to the full" (John 10:10). I chose that night to do life God's way and only his way, and to live according to his amazing guidelines in his beautiful Bible.

Finally, I gave Jesus permission to be back in my life. I asked him to guide me and correct me. I surrendered to him.

I don't know if you believe in God or miracles, but the next day I woke up and it was the first day in two years I didn't make myself sick! The next day, week, month, year—and to this day—I have never made myself sick. God had taken this illness from me which I and no doctor could do in just one night. I started reading the Bible again and decided to believe what God said about me, not what the world said. God said I was precious, fearfully and wonderfully made, worth everything to him. I was LOVED!

I have never turned back on that prayer. Since then,

I can testify that God has given me an adventure—more than I could have dreamed or imagined. I wanted to serve God so I signed up with the children's team at my local church and saw how God could use me to share his amazing love with others. I then joined a national children's team called Powerpoint. That's where I met my now husband Tim. Tim was a dancer and rapper, and before I knew it, we moved to Manchester, England and joined The World Wide Message Tribe (a dance band who shared the most amazing Gospel, the greatest display of love ever, in schools).

Somehow our music took off and we got a U.K. and an American recording contract. Shortly afterward, I was doing an interview with a radio station and in walked Luis Palau himself—the guy who introduced me to a personal God 15 years earlier. He's my spiritual dad and we saw each other at events regularly. God is so good! Since then, I have spent a decade being a television presenter, capturing God on the move in lives around the world. I'm also the founder and manager of a ministry called Respect Me which is part of The Message Trust family. We send teams around the world into schools teaching God's love, acceptance, and value. We also inform, equip, and empower young people to make not just good but God choices with their lives.

This may all sound exciting and yes, it is! But sometimes, it's the smaller things that blow me away…the fact that God didn't forget my desire to hear those three words from my dad. It may have taken 30 years, a bottle of wine, and some discussion, but my dad finally told me he loved me! I love my dad massively and I know he loves me. He just shows me rather than using words.

Finally, back to music. I have to admit that my favorite song of all time has to be by Chaka Khan, "Ain't Nobody Loves Me Better."

No one—not even your parents, bestie, your girl- or boyfriend, or even your dog—can ever love you more or better than God does. Why don't you give him a chance to love you today?

Scripture says, "For God so loved the world that he gave his one and only Son, that whoever believes in him shall not perish but have eternal life" (John 3:16).

THE GREATEST DISPLAY OF LOVE EVER!

*Emma and her husband live in the U.K. with their three children. She is the founder of a nonprofit that seeks to equip, empower, and build-up young people.*

# NOT
# THE END

WENDY

As I write this, I am sitting in the basement of my home in Portland, Oregon, quarantined from my family. I have COVID-19. I can't believe I was the only one in my immediate family to get this dreaded virus, and I can't figure out where I contracted it. But as my body heals and I patiently wait for it to gain full strength once again, I am thinking about hope.

Our world has been in a position of hopelessness and fear for more than a year. Many are sick. Many…too many… have died. The economy is struggling. Many have lost jobs. And there is a mounting mental-health crisis among the younger generation, a tidal wave of soul misery, that will probably only get worse as time goes on.

Things feel hopeless.

Yet, here I sit. And I don't feel hopeless. And it's not because things are great.

I don't feel hopeless because I know this world is not my home. We were never promised easy days on our life journey. In fact, we were actually promised the opposite. So why are we surprised?

Is it possible to still have hope in the midst of these circumstances? I believe the answer is a resounding, "YES!" And that is exactly why I compiled these stories. These are true accounts from some amazing women…of hope found despite sometimes unbearable circumstances.

I wonder if, as you read these stories, they brought to mind your own story. Your own discouragement, despair, disappointment, or agonizing past. My friend, if nothing else, I want you to know you can also have hope. Despite the chaos of a global pandemic. Despite your past. Despite your mistakes or your failures. Anything you have done of which you are ashamed. Despite what others have done to you…you can have hope!

As I said in the introduction…hope is found in a person. And not just any person. One person. Jesus Christ.

I don't know what you think about Jesus. You've probably heard his name. But have you ever wondered what he could really mean to you personally?

Maybe you believe Jesus belongs in a church. Or maybe he's up in the sky somewhere. Maybe you struggle to believe that he actually is who he claimed to be…God…come to earth as a man.

Jesus walked here on earth thousands of years ago. It's all recorded in the first four books of the New Testament. Firsthand accounts by those who witnessed it. His friends, Matthew, Mark, Luke and John.

I encourage you to read about Jesus. You might have ideas about him. But have you really read the account of his life? What did he actually say? How did he interact with people? The poor? The powerful? His family? His friends? What about his kindness and compassion? Or his radical, upside-down ways that point people away from pious, dead religious chasing around, and toward an authentic, honest relationship with God? He showed us a different way. A vibrant way that results in joy, possibility, and hope.

The most radical thing Jesus did—the act that yields these hopeful results—is that he died. He gave his life willingly. He let the authorities take him, accuse him, lie about him, and ultimately crucify him. And he did it because of his love for humanity and his obedience to his Father—God, the Creator.

Jesus gave his life—taking the sins of the world on himself. The Bible calls him the perfect lamb that was slain for the sins of the world.

But, that is not the end of the story. Three days after he was murdered, Jesus—beautiful, kind, powerful Jesus—rose from the dead. He came back from death to life! And he is the only one who could do that because he is the only true God.

Because of this miraculous act…all those years ago… you and I can have life and hope and healing.

Read these words for yourself:

> *"…it was our weakness He carried;*
> *It was our sorrows that weighed Him down.*

*And we thought His troubles were a punishment*
     *from God,*
*A punishment for His own sins!*
*But He was pierced for our rebellion,*
*Crushed for our sins.*
*He was beaten so we could be whole.*
*He was whipped so we could be healed.*
*All of us, like sheep, have strayed away.*
*We have left God's paths to follow our own.*
*Yet the Lord laid on Him the sins of us all…"*
Isaiah 53 (NLT)

I hope that shocks you just as it does me. I encourage you to ask God right now to help you, to clarify to you, in your mind and spirit, just what that means for you and your life. What do you do with that precious, amazing, wonderful gift that has been given to you? Do you take it, accept it, and enjoy it? Or do you reject it? I pray you see it as personally as I do. That God knew you needed him. He sees the chasm between you and him. And he was willing to make this type of sacrifice for you!

My friend, you can receive this gift for yourself. This truth. Not in some abstract, religious way. But in a true, authentic, and personal way. You can actually talk to God right now, wherever you are, as you read these words.

You can reach out to God. Call out audibly! Or even in your thoughts…in your heart. You can ask him right now to be your Lord…your Savior…your King. You can ask him to take control of your life…once and for all. He will amend your story. The next chapters of your life. The conclusion. It can all be written in a new and hopeful way…just like the women in this book.

*He is calling you.*
*Come, come…*
*If you are thirsty, come.*
*And take the free gift of the water of life.*

If you would like to do this, below are some simple words. Not magic words in any sense. Just a simple prayer… your heart connecting to the Living God:

*Jesus…*
*Thank you.*
*Thank you for never giving up on me.*
*Thank you for loving me.*
*I hear you speaking to me, and I respond to you now.*
*Thank you for dying, for taking the punishment*
*        for all my garbage.*
*Thank you for being powerful enough to rise again.*
*Clean me out.*
*Help me Lord to live for you.*
*I can't do this alone.*
*Give me the power to walk with you.*
*Not perfect, but changing day by day.*

*My life is yours.*
*Amen. Amen!*

Oh friend, even as I am writing this, I have tears. To imagine you praying this to the Living God. What a joy! Wherever you might be in the world, I am celebrating with you. Oh, I know he has so much joy to receive you as his own. He's been calling you for a long time!

I would love to hear from you. To know of your decision to follow Jesus. It truly would give me the greatest joy to know if you prayed this prayer to commit your life to walk with Jesus. Would you do me a favor and send me an email at wendy@palau.org? I will commit to praying for you. For your new life in Christ.

And as you walk with him, I pray you will dig into his word—the Bible. And connect with his people—the Church.

I pray the Lord continues to speak to you and guide you. I know he will, as you listen to his voice and follow his words. And I pray that your story, as the Lord continues to write it, will be used to bless others, just like these stories have blessed you.

Jesus didn't promise us an easy life. But he did promise us a good life as we follow him. And he promised to fill us with his hope…each and every day.

God bless you, my friend.

# SHARE YOUR STORY

Nothing would encourage us more than to hear from you. We want to know how this book had an impact on you, but even more, we want to know how God spoke to you through the stories in this book.

You can connect with Wendy Palau, or any of the women in this book, by sending an email to wendy@palau.org.

You may also connect with the larger ministry of the Luis Palau Association via:

| | |
|---|---|
| Web: | www.palau.org |
| Phone: | 888.877.5847 |
| Facebook: | www.facebook.com/LuisPalauLive |
| Instagram: | www.instagram.com/LuisPalauLive |